Stakeholder Engagement

Stakeholder Engagement

Improving Education through Multilevel Community Relations

Edited by
Henry Tran, Douglas A. Smith, and
David G. Buckman

ROWMAN & LITTLEFIELD
Lanham • Boulder • New York • London

Published by Rowman & Littlefield
An imprint of The Rowman & Littlefield Publishing Group, Inc.
4501 Forbes Boulevard, Suite 200, Lanham, Maryland 20706
www.rowman.com

6 Tinworth Street, London SE11 5AL, United Kingdom

Copyright © 2020 by Henry Tran, Douglas A. Smith, and David G. Buckman

All rights reserved. No part of this book may be reproduced in any form or by any electronic or mechanical means, including information storage and retrieval systems, without written permission from the publisher, except by a reviewer who may quote passages in a review.

British Library Cataloguing in Publication Information Available

Library of Congress Cataloging-in-Publication Data

Names: Tran, Henry (Professor of education finance), editor. | Smith, Douglas A. (Educational leadership professor), editor. | Buckman, David G., editor.
Title: Stakeholder engagement : improving education through multi-level community relations / Edited by Henry Tran, Douglas A. Smith, and David G. Buckman.
Description: Lanham : Lexington Books, [2020] | Includes bibliographical references. | Summary: "This book focuses on the topic of the multiple-stakeholders that comprise the education community across the P-20 continuum"— Provided by publisher.
Identifiers: LCCN 2019042323 (print) | LCCN 2019042324 (ebook) |
    ISBN 9781475854886 (cloth) | ISBN 9781475854893 (paperback) |
    ISBN 9781475854909 (epub)
Subjects: LCSH: School improvement programs. | Educational planning. | Educational leadership.
Classification: LCC LB2822.8 .S68 2020 (print) | LCC LB2822.8 (ebook) | DDC 371.2/07—dc23
LC record available at https://lccn.loc.gov/2019042323
LC ebook record available at https://lccn.loc.gov/2019042324

Contents

Editorial Introduction · vii

PART I: P-12 · 1

1. Voices from the Field Commentary: The Importance of Effectively Communicating with All Stakeholders: Utilizing Technology to Engage the School-wide Community · 3
   Denver J. Fowler

2. The Accuracy of a Reductionist Message: A Case Study of Public Relations Involving a Michigan K-12 School Bond Referendum · 11
   Alan J. Brokaw, Erin L. Merz, and Thomas E. Merz

3. The Importance of Shared Vision and Stakeholder Influence on K-12 School Leaders' Efforts to Improve Student Mathematics Achievement · 33
   Emma P. Bullock and Patricia S. Moyer-Packenham

4. School Leaders' Reflective Blogs Inspire Systemic Change: A Narrative Inquiry · 59
   Rita J. Hartman, Cheryl Burleigh, and James Lane

5. Resettled Muslim Parents' Perceptions of School-Community Relations · 77
   Michael E. Hess, Charles L. Lowery, Rowda Olad, Connor Fewell, Steven Yeager, and Tracy Kondrit

6	Book Review: Partnering with Parents to Ask the Right Questions by Santana Luz, Dan Rothstein, and Agnes Bain *Art Stellar*	99

PART II: HIGHER EDUCATION — 103

7	How Can Higher Education Engage with Rural Communities to Address Their Teacher Shortages? *Henry Tran and Theresa Harrison*	105
8	Systemic Advocacy and Stakeholder Collaborations: Supporting Students Emerging from Foster Care Who Matriculate to College *Sarah Jones*	121
9	Prime Real Estate: Branding University Syllabi *Vickie Shamp Ellis, Kaylene Barbe, Ann McNellis, and Braden East*	135
10	Engaging Industry Stakeholders: A Case Study of Academic Assessment Practice at a Rural Agricultural Focused Two-Year College *Douglas A. Smith, Emily C. Fox, and Alexander T. Jordan*	149

About the Authors — 165

Editorial Introduction

There is an old African proverb that says "it takes a village to raise a child." Relatedly, it takes a community of people to educate a person. This book focuses on the topic of the multiple stakeholders that comprise the education community across the P-20 continuum. In various ways and forms, the authors of the chapters found within this book promote the importance of engaging with the diverse array of stakeholders in order to truly improve education in an increasingly interconnected world.

The book itself is divided into two major arcs, the first of which covers community relations and stakeholder engagement in P-12 schools, while the second addresses those same issues in higher education. To lead effectively in P-12 schools, it is essential to consider the voice of stakeholders in decision-making and promote opportunities for stakeholder engagement.

Schools can impact stakeholders at multiple levels, and, conversely, the stakeholders can also impact schools. Thus, without the inclusion of stakeholder involvement in decisions that affect the community at large, institutions can fail to provide quality educational services that meet the diverse array of needs of the broader educational community and run the risk of alienating potential sources of support.

The term "stakeholder" is interpreted broadly. Stakeholder involvement in P-12 schools includes, but is not limited to: students, parents, educators, higher education institutions, businesses, multicultural representatives, and government officials. This multilevel community structure can also be viewed as a multitiered structure of support, whereby schools and districts develop relationships with stakeholders and gain capital (e.g., social, political, and financial) to propel their school forward academically and address the needs of all students.

Feedback and engagement from these individuals provide quality control structures, promote ingenuity, builds advocacy, and offer perspectives that may not be represented on the school board or school leadership team. As such, the aforementioned benefits of strong community relations and stakeholder involvement ensures the educational environment within the school is reflective of and addresses the needs of the broader community, which can essentially better serve students and promote positive educational outcomes.

On the higher education side, stakeholders are likewise multiple and wide ranging. These individuals and groups are affected by what colleges and universities do and produce. Stakeholders internal to higher education prominently include students, faculty, and staff and externally include communities, employers, alumni, and government agencies. These multiple stakeholders often have differing expectations and often create an environment in which institutional leaders are forced to negotiate and balance competing demands.

Stakeholder engagement in higher education is important to organize and facilitate support for institutions to fulfill their missions. In part, this requires an understanding of who stakeholders are internally and externally, understanding their needs, listening, and engaging them appropriately.

In higher education, it is important for leaders, faculty, and staff to understand the complexity of engaging multiple stakeholders. Through this book, we provide a sample of stakeholder engagement in higher education to begin constructing the picture of the complex universe of stakeholders and how institutions interact with them to meet the needs of students and communities.

When one considers the activities that take place within education institutions, there is a realization that they are influenced and driven by much more than just the educators and administrators who occupy the schools. In the editors' own work, (e.g., see Tran & Bon, 2016; Buckman, & Johnson, & Alexander, 2018), the importance of the inclusion of the viewpoints and inputs of multiple stakeholders in school decisions when appropriate has been consistently argued, given that the school is considered by many to be a social and communal environment.

To address these issues, in this text, this book is lucky to have a collection of peer-reviewed writing that explores various aspects of how multiple stakeholder input can be used to improve school decisions.

The initial chapters cover several relevant subjects that include (1) the importance of effective engagement and communication with multiple stakeholders within the school community, (2) the importance of engaging with the public when seeking financial support from the community, (3) the importance of shared vision and stakeholder influence on K-12 school leaders, (4) how students can influence school leadership decisions and directions, and (5) how to engage and communicate with an increasingly diverse school community.

The next set of chapters starts with a gateway piece that bridges P-12 to higher education. These second set of chapters cover topics such as: (1) how higher education can engage with rural communities, (2) internal and external education stakeholder engagement, (3) the role of course syllabi as a mechanism for student communication and stakeholder engagement, and (4) the role industry stakeholders have in assessment practices.

In the end, hopefully, this book helps readers broaden their view of who they might consider as relevant stakeholders and understand how institutions might leverage their capacity to improve education.

Sincerely,

Henry Tran
Douglas A. Smith
David Buckman

REFERENCES

Buckman, D. G., Johnson, A. D., & Alexander, D. (2018). Internal versus external promotion: Advancement of teachers to administrators. *Journal of Educational Administration, 56*(1), 33–49.

Tran, H., & Bon, S. (2016). Principal quality and selection: Including multiple stakeholders' perspectives. *Journal of School Public Relations, 37*(1), 55–78.

Part I

P-12

Chapter 1

Voices from the Field Commentary

The Importance of Effectively Communicating with All Stakeholders: Utilizing Technology to Engage the School-wide Community

Denver J. Fowler

Perhaps, now more than ever, the need to effectively engage and communicate with the school community is vital to the livelihood of a given school or district, particularly as it applies to increasing school community involvement and fostering a positive school climate and culture. This communication certainly plays a role in such constructs, and due to the rise of affordable and readily accessible technology, school leaders and teachers can easily communicate in real time with all stakeholders, including students, staff, parents, community members, and business owners (Epstein, 2011; Fowler, 2018; Sanchez, 2018; Schneider & Coleman, 1993).

The opportunity to effectively engage the school community within a given school building or district can be achieved somewhat effortlessly in the twenty-first century, and there is little doubt that schools who do not engage the school community will most likely be those schools who have a negative school climate and culture and, furthermore, are unsuccessful in increasing school community and parental involvement (Blackburn & Williamson, 2018; Epstein et al., 2019; Fowler, 2018; Gonder & Hymes, 1994).

In addition, and perhaps worth mentioning, the use of such technology to communicate with the school community becomes especially important in schools that serve a majority of students who are considered to be of low socioeconomic status.

Ungarino (2015) reported that for more and more poor Americans, smartphones are lifelines, and such individuals check their smartphones dozens more times in a single day than the average user. Such groups of individuals included those to be considered to have low income and education levels, are nonwhite, and are young adults.

Thus, the best way to engage and communicate with such individuals may be through the use of technology (including social media) with regard to all things school. Therefore, to this end, the aim of this commentary will be to highlight the educational technology available to school leaders and teachers and how these individuals might utilize such technology to effectively communicate and engage the school community, while being cognizant of the aforementioned benefits of such communication.

EDUCATIONAL TECHNOLOGY IN THE TWENTY-FIRST CENTURY

It was reported that $8.15 billion was invested in educational technology companies in the first ten months of 2017 alone (Emmanuel, 2018). Thus, as one can imagine, the question is no longer whether or not the technology exists, but rather, which technology to use—as it applies to engaging the school community, more specifically, the stakeholders, in which a given school serves, including students, staff, parents, community members, and business owners. In the following sections, some of the preeminent educational technology (including Apps and social media) that school leaders and teachers can utilize on a regular basis to communicate with and effectively engage the school community have been highlighted.

EDUCATIONAL TECHNOLOGY FOR SCHOOL LEADERS AND TEACHERS

Although as one might fathom, there is a vast amount of educational technology for both school leaders and teachers to choose from. However, what was found in an in-depth research on such educational technology, Apps, and social media is that not one form of the technology is necessarily better than the other. In fact, on the contrary, the best school leaders and teachers utilize an array of educational technology to ensure they are engaging all stakeholders through a variety of modes, offering the pertinent information in a variety of forms, with the end goal of guaranteeing that all stakeholders have equal access to such information.

Thus, it might be that the best approach for both school leaders and teachers is to build relationships with all stakeholders and, in doing so, determine what educational technology, Apps, and social media such stakeholders are already using and most easily able to regularly access. In doing so, school leaders and teachers can help ensure they are effectively communicating with the school community and, thus, foster a positive school climate and culture, while increasing community and parental involvement.

Educational Technology for School Leaders

As previously mentioned, there are numerous forms of educational technology for school leaders. Thus, several forms of educational technology, Apps, and social media that school leaders should find useful for effectively communicating with and engaging the school community have been highlighted (See table 1.1). In addition, the *name, where to find it, how to use it*, and *notes* are included (Fowler, 2018). To be clear, it may go without mentioning that the educational technology, Apps, and social media shared in table 1.1 could and can be utilized by teachers and other school staff as well. This particular aspect applies to both tables 1 and 2.

Educational Technology for School Teachers

In table 1.2, several forms of educational technology, Apps, and social media that school teachers should find useful for effectively communicating with and engaging the school community are highlighted. In addition, the *name, where to find it, how to use it,* and *notes* are included (Fowler, 2018). Again, to be clear, it may go without mentioning that the educational technology, Apps, and social media shared could and can be utilized by teachers and other school staff as well. This particular aspect applies to both the tables.

As you can see, there are multiple forms of educational technology, Apps, and social media that can be utilized to effectively communicate and engage the school community. Additionally, with recently created Apps such as Hootsuite, this communication can be managed from one dashboard, allowing our all-too-busy school leaders and teachers to effortlessly and regularly communicate with the stakeholders in which they serve. In doing so, schools can help ensure all stakeholders are involved in the process of educating our students. This communication undoubtedly builds a sense of community among all stakeholders, helps foster a positive school climate and culture, and helps increase community and parent involvement.

Table 1.1 Educational Technology for School Leaders

Name	Where to Find It	How to Use It	Notes
Twitter	App or Twitter.com	Create a district/building/classroom Twitter account. Tweet about everything—celebrate everything and celebrate often!	Lingo is "Follow" our Twitter handle. Use hashtag to connect all tweets.
Facebook	App or Facebook.com	Create a district/building/classroom Facebook page. Post about everything—celebrate everything and celebrate often!	Lingo is "Like" our Facebook page. Use hashtag to promote your hashtag. Post images, videos, and so on.
Instagram	App or Instagram.com	Create a district/building/classroom Instagram feed. Post images/videos about everything and celebrate it all!	Lingo is "Follow" our Instagram feed. Use hashtags and include link by asking followers to "swipe up" (business account).
LinkedIn	App or LinkedIn.com	Create a LinkedIn Group for all stakeholders to join on LinkedIn.	Lingo is to "Join" our LinkedIn Group. It is a great way to keep all stakeholders connected (and alum).
SonarCloud	App or GetSonarCloud.com	Make PA announcements from anywhere, anytime to all stakeholders.	Best part, real time translation (to most all languages).
Voxer	App or Voxer.com	Turns your smartphone into a walkie-talkie to connect with select groups or all stakeholders.	Great for emergency situations, no longer need to worry about range of walkie-talkies.
Hootsuite	App or Hootsuite.com	Control all of your district, building, and classroom social media from one place.	Schedule tweets, posts, pics, etc., from one place.

Note. Although this list of Apps and social media is geared toward school leaders, all school staff can utilize this technology to further communicate with all stakeholders.

Table 1.2 Educational Technology for School Teachers

Name	Where to Find It	How to Use It	Notes
Remind101	App or Remind101.com	Communicate (send reminders) to all stakeholders via one App.	Include parents in the learning and send a reminder now and then.
ClassDojo	App or ClassDojo.com	Create a positive classroom environment while also ensuring you call on all students.	Post student "stories" to share with parents and other stakeholders in the community.
Edmodo	Edmodo.com	It is a Learning Management System (LMS). You are preparing your students for college and parents can access it as well.	Get students (and parents) college ready by using this LMS (much like Blackboard, Canvas, etc.) in your classroom.
Teacher Aide Pro	App or Teacher AidePro.com	Teachers can track and share attendance, seating charts, data, and more with parents, students, and other school staff.	No need for a hard copy gradebook, seating chart, etc., track it all by smartphone or iPad (or the like).
Swivl	App or Swivl.com	Teachers can record lessons, student presentations, and so on, and share with students, parents, and other community members.	Also a great tool to document observations. Wear necklace/mic that is tracked by the Swivl device (no need to stand in one place, it will follow. you).

Note. Although this list of Apps and social media is geared toward school teachers, all school staff can utilize this technology to further communicate with all stakeholders.

FINAL THOUGHTS

As the chief focus (and perhaps main benefits) of effectively communicating with and engaging the school community is this idea of fostering a positive school climate and culture, and, furthermore, increasing community and parent involvement. As such, it might be beneficial to include some specifics as it applies to each.

First and foremost, as a school leader and teacher, ideal of "telling your schools story, don't let others tell it for you" is highly recommended. For example, in a recent study by Henry (2017), it was determined that the majority of superintendents agreed that educational technology should be used to deliver positive messages that highlight their respective school districts.

To this end, a school leader and teacher must constantly celebrate all of the wonderful things happening throughout their school as well as within their classrooms—every day and every class period. This can be accomplished through the educational technology, Apps, and social media shared in this commentary. In essence, by doing so, you are branding your school. To be frank, do not let the state assessment results define your school—as we educators know there is so much more to a school than test scores. Celebrate it all, and celebrate it often.

Secondly, leaders must ensure their schools are truly "community schools." This can be accomplished by rethinking how our schools operate and how they can better be woven into the fabric of the community in which it serves. It is here that our schools become centers of the community and are open to everyone—all day, every day, evenings, and weekends. A place where partnerships are formed, and schools become a place for opportunities for all stakeholders including students, staff, parents, community members, and business owners to learn, grow, and reach their full potential.

Finally, if the central goal is for school leaders and teachers to effectively and regularly communicate with all stakeholders, such individuals must first build relationships with said stakeholders, in an effort to learn what ways such individuals are accessing information via educational technology, Apps, and social media. Only then can the best mode of communication for our stakeholders be determined, and then the information be utilized to ensure leaders are engaging the school community in an effort to foster a positive school climate and culture and increase both community and parental involvement.

In this day and age, the majority of our stakeholders are digital natives,[1] and many (if not all) expect school leaders and teachers to be well versed in the most current and effective educational technology, Apps, and social media available, many of which such stakeholders are familiar with and regularly use. Thus, those in the educational setting might consider it professional malpractice to not change when they know better ways of doing things.

Furthermore, in more recent years, there has certainly been a clear divide as it relates to schools in today's world (Casas, Whitaker, & Zoul, 2015). Quite simply, generally speaking, there are two types of schools that exist in today's world, those who are preparing students for the future and those that are allowing adults to live comfortably in the past (Kieschnick, 2018).

There is little doubt as to what is the key difference between such schools; simply put, there are those schools who utilize technology in all that they do (including communication with the school community and their stakeholders) and those who do not support (and in some cases even ban per policy) technology in their schools. In the twenty-first century, school leaders and teachers must embrace technology and utilize it to effectively engage the school community in an effort to foster a positive school climate and culture while increasing community and parent involvement. To do otherwise, is no less than malpractice.

NOTE

1. A digital native is an individual who was born and/or brought up during the age of digital technology and is therefore familiar with computers and the Internet from an early age.

REFERENCES

Blackburn, B., & Williamson, R. (2018). Leading change in your school: A sustainable process. *Australian Educational Leader, 40*(1), 8–12.

Casas, J., Whitaker, T., & Zoul, J. (2015). *What connected educators do differently.* New York, NY: Routledge.

Emmanuel, N. (2018). *Education technology is a global opportunity.* TechCrunch. Retrieved from: https://techcrunch.com/2018/01/19/education-technology-is-a-global-opportunity/.

Epstein, J. (2011). *School, family, and community partnerships; Preparing educators and improving schools* (2nd ed.). New York, NY: Routledge.

Epstein, J., Sanders, M., Sheldon, S., Simon, B., Salinas, K., Jansorn, N., Voorhis, F., Martin, C., Thomas, B., Greenfeld, M., Hutchins, D., & Williams, K. (2019). *School, family, and community partnerships; Your handbook for action* (4th ed.). Thousand Oaks, CA: Corwin.

Fowler, D. (2018). *The 21st century school leader: Leading schools in today's world.* Ontario, Canada: Word & Deed Publishing.

Gonder, P. O., & Hymes, D. (1994). Improving school climate and culture. *AASA Critical Issues Report, 27,* 1–123.

Henry, J. (2017). Social media use. *School Administrator, 8*(75), 43–44.

Kieschnick, W. (2018). Teaching keating with weston and molly kieschnick. Podcast. Retrieved from: https://www.coachweston.com.

Sanchez, C. (2018). Parental involvement after the implementation of effective communication practices in a low income, high English learner populated school in California: A case study. *Scholarworks at CSUSM Library*, 1–57.

Schneider, B., & Coleman, J. (1993). *Parents, their children, and schools*. New York, NY: Routledge.

Ungarino, R. (2015). *For more poor Americans, smartphones are lifelines*. CNBC. Retrieved from: http://www.cnbc.com/2015/04/01/for-more-poor-americans-smart phones-are-lifelines.html.

Chapter 2

The Accuracy of a Reductionist Message

A Case Study of Public Relations Involving a Michigan K-12 School Bond Referendum

Alan J. Brokaw, Erin L. Merz, and Thomas E. Merz

Note: We thank Citizens' Committee members, Robert Bishop and Lois Jambekar, for insights on the 2017 referendum campaign; Mark Mohammadpour, APR of Edelman Portland, and Elizabeth Reed for comments on an earlier draft; Houghton County Clerk, Jennifer Lorenz, The Charter Township of Portage Supervisor, Bruce Petersen, City of Houghton assistant city manager, Ann Vollrath, and City of Houghton tax assessors, Jim Fedie, and Scott MacInnes, for helping with data collection. We are grateful to two anonymous reviewers for their careful reading and comments. The views expressed in this paper are entirely our own.

Abstract: This study examines the public relations surrounding a 2017 Michigan K-12 school bond referendum. The school board and the internal activist Citizens' Committee's reductionist message that the referendum's cost to the average household was about $4.45 each month, or the cost of two cups of coffee, probably lowered the likelihood of widespread sticker shock among voters. The public relations' precise language and imagery, while not entirely accurate, no doubt contributed to the campaign's success. The lesson learned from this study is that, in school bond referendums, avoiding the inaccuracy described here will likely diminish the possibility of publics suspecting the school board, school administrators, and internal activists of intentionally disseminating misinformation.

THE ACCURACY OF A REDUCTIONIST MESSAGE: A CASE STUDY OF PUBLIC RELATIONS INVOLVING A MICHIGAN K-12 SCHOOL BOND REFERENDUM

Thinking of public relations only from the perspective of corporations and business interests, however, ignores the reality that activist organizations and groups strategically use communication efforts to call attention to, frame, and advocate issues, positions and activities.—Ciszek, 2015

But it's important to remember that people gather statistics. People choose what to count, how to go about counting, which of the resulting numbers they will share with us, and which words they will use to describe and interpret those numbers.—Levitin, 2016

In 2017–2018, Michigan had 545 conventional K-12 public school districts (Michigan Department of Education, 2018). Conventional districts are comprised of a single local governmental unit, such as a city or township, or are a joint district comprised of more than one local governmental unit. One thing they had in common was limits on how much money each district could borrow without asking voters (DeGrow, 2017). Seeking voter approval can involve a district's school board, school administration, and local citizen groups conducting public relations aimed at influencing thoughts and behaviors of publics.

This case study focuses on a Michigan school district's most recent qualified bond referendums, 2016 and 2017.[1] Voters rejected the former and approved the latter. Consistent with situational theory of publics, members of the 2017 citizens' volunteer committee: (1) recognized the issue (approving the referendum) and knew what needed to be done—primarily getting yes voters to vote, (2) faced no opposing organized activist group, and (3) had a close connection between themselves and the issue—"the issue had salience" (Ciszek, 2015, p. 449). Committee members operated as internal activists whose objective was congruous rather than conflicting with that of the school board. Thus, our case study differs from that of Curtin (2016), which examined the internal activism of two Girl Scouts and their reductionist message that Girl Scout cookies kill orangutans. The two Scouts sought removal of palm oil from Girl Scout cookies *against* the wish of the organization, Girl Scouts USA. "The organization's discourse distanced the [two] Scouts from itself and itself from the issue" (Curtin, 2016, p. 24).

Our study links the two opening literary epigraphs. To foreshadow this linkage, the public relations of the school board and the Citizens' Committee regarding the 2017 proposal's cost to the taxpayers was examined for precision and accuracy. "Precision reflects the exactitude with which we can express something," and "accuracy is a measure of whether a figure is broadly consistent with the truth" (Wheelan, 2013, p. 37).

The genesis of this study was the authors' curiosity surrounding the accuracy of a precise descriptive statistic, the average homeowner's monthly tax increase, widely communicated to gain voter approval of the 2017 proposal. Perhaps more influential in gaining voter approval was the adoption of an often-used public relations tactic in the domain of charitable donations—the Citizens' Committee conveyed the reductionist message that voter approval would result in homeowners sacrificing "about the price of two cups of coffee per month." We found this message lacked information that perhaps would have aided voters in formulating questions and in making decisions that were more informed.

THE 2016 QUALIFIED BOND PROPOSAL

On May 3, 2016, voters in the Houghton-Portage Township Schools District (henceforth, District) located in Michigan's Upper Peninsula went to the polls voting on a bonding proposal for the District to borrow a sum not to exceed $8.69 million. The joint District is comprised of two municipalities, the City of Houghton and Portage Township. The 2016 ballot stated the bonds were to be issued for the purpose of:

> Remodeling, equipping and re-equipping and furnishing and re-furnishing school buildings; erecting, furnishing and equipping a press box and a concession stand addition to the fieldhouse; and preparing, developing, improving and equipping play fields, athletic fields and facilities and sites. [The 2016 ballot is found in exhibit 4.]

Prior to voting day the District's Board of Education (henceforth, Board) posted an informational document on the District's web page titled "Frequently Asked Questions" and held two public forums. The web page and the forums informed residents of the need for infrastructure improvements and the project's cost. A search by the authors of the local newspaper, *The Daily Mining Gazette* (henceforth, *DMG*), revealed no feature articles or letters to the editor related to the proposal thirty days prior to voting day. There were a few posts on social media opposing the proposal. Opposition focused on athletics—the installing of artificial turf on the high school's football field and building a press box. Nevertheless, the proposal was not a district-wide topic of conversation. A worker at one of the city's polling stations informed the authors that perhaps a dozen individuals entered the station simply because they were driving by and saw the sign "Vote Here." These passersby were clueless as to why voting was occurring. Poll workers instructed them to examine the posted ballot. Upon doing so, some of the heretofore-clueless passersby proceeded to vote.

The lack of mass-media attention suggests that the proposal "flew under the radar." Perhaps the Board believed that those who were most aware of the proposal—teachers, school administrators, parents of school-aged children—were closely allied to the school and would be yes voters. If "flying under the radar" was a chosen strategy, it failed to deliver the intended outcome. The proposal was narrowly defeated 338 (50.5%) No to 331 (49.5%) Yes (see table 2.1). The proposal passed in the city with 52.2 percent voting Yes, but was defeated in the township with 54.7 percent voting No. The failed proposal probably shocked some individuals given the string of four prior successes (see table 2.2). However, the District was not alone. Statewide fifty-four separate qualified school bond referendums were held in 2016. Seventeen (31%) failed (Michigan Department of Treasury, 2018a).

THE 2017 QUALIFIED BOND PROPOSAL

There are plenty of recommendations on how to proceed in order to increase the likelihood of success following the defeat of a school bond proposal (Hanover, 2012; Holt, 2009; Holt, Wendt, & Smith, 2006). In such an environment, a public relations consultant hired by a school district might suggest a three-prong approach to gain voter approval. First, reframe the proposal shifting the emphasis away from athletic turf and a press box to essentials—educational and safety infrastructure improvements—while stressing the benefits to the children and the community. Second, "Consider carefully not only the amount of the [tax] increase but also the perception of the public to the amount of the increase" (Holt, Wendt, & Smith, 2006, p. 17). Third, utilize Citizens' Committee to "educate" (inculcate?) voters and to get yes voters to vote.

Table 2.1 2016 Vote Counts and Voter Turnout Rates

Location	Yes	No	Total	Voter Turnout Rates
City	212	194	406	0.153
Township	119	144	263	0.109
District	331	338	669	0.138

Source: Clerk's Office Houghton County Michigan.

Table 2.2 District Successful Bond Proposals

Date	Number of Yes Votes	Number of No Votes	Borrowing Cap ($ millions)
August 2008	635	339	12.2
April 1996	753	420	10.0
October 1987	1,208	530	6.6^
October 1987	955	783	0.90^^

Sources: Houghton-Portage Township School District and Michigan Department of Treasury (2018a). ^For construction of a new high school. ^^ For construction of a swimming pool within the new high school (assuming voters approved the new high school).

Reframing the Issue

In the fall of 2016, the Board held two public forums receiving input on possible infrastructure improvements to be included in a revised bond proposal. A November 23, 2016, front-page *DMG* article reported:

- "[Based on the comments voiced at two public forums, the Board] identified five main areas of concern: the need for better traffic flow at the elementary school; a desire to have the city's athletic facilities serve the broader facilities [sic]; for the [athletic] facilities to be available for physical education classes; the importance of remaining current on security and technology; and seeking to contain costs."
- "The proposal will include a plan to built [sic] an alternate route for elementary school drop-offs to alleviate congestion in the elementary school parking lot."
- "When voters in Houghton and Portage Township vote on a new school bond proposal in May, it'll have a larger dollar value than the one that failed last year but cost less in property taxes due to refunding existing bonds." [Authors' note: refunding made sense since current interest rates were lower than rates on the District's existing debt.]

At a January 2017 meeting, the Board set May 2 as the date for requesting voter approval to borrow a sum not to exceed $10.89 million. Thus, the requested borrowing cap exceeded that of the 2016 proposal ($8.69 mil). Hanover (2012) profiles five school districts that suffered bond referendum defeats followed up by successes. In four of the victories, the cap amount was lowered while in the fifth it remained the same. Refunding of existing debt notwithstanding, the District's request for more while recently having been denied less was a risky strategy.

As voting day approached, the bond proposal was flying well within the range of radar. On March 21, 2017, the *DMG* reported, "School board members tour district to see bond issue needs." Informational forums were held at the high school on April 10 and 21, 2017. The District's web page (http://hpts.us/) included language from the 2017 ballot describing the proposal's benefits:

> Remodeling, equipping and re-equipping, and furnishing and refurnishing school buildings; *erecting an exit canopy for the elementary school* and a concession building and new bleacher system with press box for the middle/high school; *acquiring, installing and equipping or re-equipping the middle/high school building for instructional technology*; and preparing, developing, and improving athletic structures, athletic fields, and sites, *including a new elementary school pickup/drop-off driveway*. [Italics added. Posting no longer available. Screenshot available from authors upon request. The 2017 ballot is found in the exhibit 4.]

Italicized text denotes additions relative to the 2016 ballot language. These additions are consistent with the best practices of emphasizing educational infrastructure and safety issues.

Cost to Homeowners

Probably the most challenging component of the Board's public relations campaign was communicating information pertaining to the proposal's projected cost to District taxpayers. Taxpayers often have little understanding of the ins and outs of bond financing and often find the topic boring. Moreover, taxpayers often have difficulty understanding their property tax bill (Michigan State University Extension, 2014). The District's web page displayed cost information to assist homeowners. Exhibit 1 replicates the posted information.

Understanding this information requires a brief discussion of Michigan property law. The assessed value of property is half of the purchase price of a house and is the initial taxable value. The taxable value can increase no faster than the rate of inflation or 5 percent, whichever is lower. As a result, the taxable value can be lower than the assessed value, especially for property not recently sold. For a recently purchased or built house (land and structure) with a total cost of \$142,500, this amount is the market (cash) value. During the first year of ownership, the taxable value of the house would be 50 percent of market value (\$71,250). To raise monies, counties, cities, townships, schools, and others, apply millage rates to the taxable value. One mill equals 1/1,000 of a dollar and the millage rate is the amount per \$1,000 of taxable value. If the rate were 0.75, the annual property taxes would be \$53.44 (=0.75*(\$71,250)/1,000), or \$4.45 per month. In July

EXHIBIT 1. COST TO DISTRICT HOMEOWNERS

Proposed *0.75 Mills* to support a $10.9 Million Bond Proposal [Italics added.]

The duration (term) of the bond referendum is 24.9 years

Market Value (thousands of $)	Taxable Value (thousands of $)	Monthly Cost to Homeowner ($)	Annual Cost to Homeowner ($)
60	30	1.88	22.5
80	40	2.50	30.00
100	50	3.13	37.50
120	60	3.75	45.00
142.5*	**71.25**	**4.45**	**53.44**
150	75	4.69	56.25
175	87.5	5.47	65.63
200	100	6.26	75.00
225	112.5	7.03	84.38
250	125	7.81	93.75

*Average home market value per city data.com.

2017, City-Data.com (the source cited at the bottom of exhibit 1) reported a 2015 average market (cash) value of $142,382 for detached houses located in the City of Houghton, which is close to the average house value of $142,500 shown in exhibit 1.

The District's web page (http://hpts.us/) also included cost language appearing on the 2017 official ballot (see Appendix):

> The estimated millage rate that will be levied for the proposed bonds *in 2017*, under current law *is .75 mills* ($0.75 on each $1,000 of taxable valuation). The maximum number of years the bonds may be outstanding, exclusive of any refunding, is twenty-five (25) years. The estimated simple average annual millage anticipated to be required to retire this bond debt is 2.50 mills ($2.50 on each $1,000 of taxable valuation) [*Emphasis* added. Posting no longer available. Screenshot available from authors upon request.]

Notice that the ballot language differed from the text "Proposed 0.75 Mills to support a $10.9 Million Bond Proposal" appearing in the rectangular heading at the top of exhibit 1. The ballot language says the millage rate levied in 2017 will be 0.75. Having read exhibit 1, one might have concluded that approving the proposal would result in an additional 0.75 mills during each of the twenty-five years. However, the ballot language reveals that such a conclusion would be incorrect. If the additional millage in at least one year is 0.75 and the average millage is 2.5, then in one or more years the additional millage must be greater than 2.5. Thus, the information in exhibit 1 was precise, but inaccurate. Exhibit 1 contained no mention of the bond proposal's *projected serial* annual increases in a homeowner's millage rates, taxable values, and tax payments. The inaccuracy calls to mind Cheng's (2017) advice: "Statistics are precisely defined, and they tell us exactly what they are defined to tell us. If we attribute more meaning to them than that, the error is ours, not theirs."

This omission also occurred when using the District's online "tax calculator" shown in exhibit 2. In part A, the authors assumed a middle-aged, able-bodied individual having an annual income of $100,000 and owning a City of Houghton homestead with a taxable value of $71,250. An income of $100,000 would have disqualified the homeowner from the Michigan Homestead Property Tax Credit.[2]

Part B displays the homeowner's "estimated total [school + nonschool] tax bill with and without the bond proposition." The last column reports an estimated annual tax increase of $53.44, which is equivalent to the value reported in exhibit 1. Unsurprisingly, the derived tax increase is sensitive to a "scale" effect—the reported estimated annual tax increase exceeded the reported monthly increase ($4.45), which exceeded the reported daily increase ($0.15). Reporting an hourly tax increase of $0.006 would have further trivialized the tax trauma.[3] Part B's "estimated tax impact analysis" was flawed because it was based solely on the 2017 additional millage rate of 0.75. The analysis ignored the other twenty-four projected millage rates if the proposal were to pass. As we will see, the set of twenty-four consisted of eight rates equaling 0.75 and sixteen rates exceeding 0.75.

Internal Activism

The Board was not alone in disseminating information about the 2017 bond proposal. The group Citizens Vote Yes for HPTS (Houghton-Portage Township Schools) Committee (henceforth, Committee) was actively engaged in getting yes voters to vote. The Committee was comprised of respectable citizens with diverse backgrounds and community roles: engineer, retired K-12 teacher, police officer, pharmacist, school psychologist, sports booster club officer, two Board members, a university professor and an emeritus university

EXHIBIT 2. THE TAX CALCULATOR

Part A

Houghton Portage Township Schools
HOMESTEAD PROPERTY TAX CREDIT MODEL

1. Please Input Your Annual Household Income. [_____]
2. Please Input Your Taxable Value (Approximately 50% Home Value). [_____]
3. If you are age 65 or older, or a spouse of a person who was 65 or older at the time of death that has not subsequently remarried select "Senior". If you are deaf, hemiplegic, paraplegic, quadriplegic, or totally and permanently disabled, select "Disabled".
   All others select General.
   - ● General
   - ○ Senior
   - ○ Disabled
4. Please select if your property is Homestead or Non-Homestead.
   - ● Homestead
   - ○ Non-Homestead
5. Please choose the appropriate Local Unit within which your property is located. (Make sure to click on the name) [City of Houghton ▼]

[Calculate Estimated Tax Impact]

Part B

Houghton Portage Township Schools
HOMESTEAD PROPERTY TAX CREDIT MODEL
Estimated Tax Impact Analysis
City of Houghton

General Claimants

	Without Bond Proposition	With Bond Proposition	Increase (Decrease)
Estimated Tax Bill	$3,165.67	$3,219.11	$53.44
Less: Homestead Property Tax Credit Available	$0.00	$0.00	$0.00
Estimated Net Tax Bill after Homestead Property Tax Credit	$3,165.67	$3,219.11	$53.44
ESTIMATED NET ANNUAL TAX INCREASE:			$53.44
ESTIMATED NET MONTHLY TAX INCREASE:			$4.45
ESTIMATED NET DAILY TAX INCREASE:			$0.15

Estimated Net Tax Increase calculated using a Taxable Value of **$71,250.00**, a Household Income of **$100,000.00**, a before Bond Proposition Millage Rate of **44.4305** (of which **8.89** mills is for existing school district debt) and a Millage Increase of **.75**. If property taxpayers itemize deductions on their federal income tax return, the taxpayer's net federal income tax will likely decrease and the "net" tax increase to the taxpayer would be less than shown above.

[Return To Input Form] [Print Results]

professor. The two Board members served as advisors to the Committee but did not participate in Committee-organized public relations activities. Other individuals assisted the Committee by canvasing neighborhoods via phone calls and door-to-door visits. Often the messenger can be more important than the message (Flynn, 2016). Thus, it is unsurprising that "[school bond] campaigns which are led by prominent community members are often more successful than campaigns driven primarily by the school board or other school officials" (Hanover, 2012, p. 3).

The Committee's campaign targeted two, not necessarily mutually exclusive, subsets of registered voters: (i) individuals most likely to vote yes and (ii) individuals receiving absentee ballots for the May 2, 2017, referendum. The Committee's orchestrated activities included door-to-door visits, phone calls, a postcard mailing, a web page, and a Facebook page. A Committee member informed the authors that the strategy was to get likely yes voters to vote rather than attempt to change the minds of likely no voters—a well-known best practice surrounding school bond referendums (Holt, 2009). What caught the attention of the authors was the postcard's cleverly worded message. Exhibit 3 replicates the message.

EXHIBIT 3. CITIZEN'S COMMITTEE POSTCARD MESSAGE

"For the price of about 2 cups of coffee a month, homeowners will:

- Improve aging and deteriorated classroom, auditorium, bathroom, and other school facilities
- Ensure better safety with a new elementary school dropoff [sic]
- Provide a reliable, updated technology for learning
- Modernize and bring our athletic facilities into compliance
- Reduce energy cost.

Vote YES for HPTS Millage Proposal Tuesday, May 2nd."

The Committee's Facebook posting stated:

- "Citizens Vote YES for HPTS is a committee of parents, volunteers, community leaders and others supporting the Houghton-Portage Township Schools May 2 bond proposal. The .75 mills requested—which will cost the average household about $4.45 each month—will address numerous problems with our school's aging facilities, safety and security needs, outdated technology and inefficient heating and ventilation systems."
- "Cost of Starbucks Unicorn Frappuccino = $4.95. Average monthly cost to Houghton taxpayers for bond proposal = $4.45 (much better investment for less money, and . . . no calories). Please vote yes on May 2nd." [Authors' note: A picture of a cup of Starbucks Unicorn Frappuccino was included. Posting no longer available. Screenshot available from authors upon request.]

Thus, the Committee's campaign strategy matched that of the Board: accentuate the essential benefits—improve infrastructure, learning, safety, compliance, and energy savings—while trivializing the cost.

Table 2.3 2017 Vote Counts and Voter Turnout Rates

Location	Yes	No	Total	Voter Turnout Rates
City	433	244	667	0.256 (67)
Township	281	247	528	0.218 (100)
District	714 (116)	491 (45)	1,205 (80)	0.238 (72)

Source: Clerk's Office Houghton County Michigan. Values in parentheses are percentage changes relative to 2016 (Table 2.1).

Using the tax calculator's monthly cost estimate for the average homeowner, "the price of about two cups of coffee a month" was $4.45, or $2.23 per cup. A coffee connoisseur might question the accuracy of this precise number lacking information on the brand of coffee, the size of the cup and location of consumption. Framing the message in terms of the price of coffee trivializes the sacrifice surrounding the act, an often-used marketing ploy in the domain of charitable giving: "By giving a dollar a day—less than the cost of a cup of coffee or Sunday newspaper—you can help alleviate suffering around the world" (Savary, Goldsmith, & Ravidhar, 2015, p. 37).

Referencing coffee can trivialize gains as well as sacrifices (Wheelan, 2013). Assume you invested in a private firm. You are informed that the firm's profits increased by 46 percent from the previous year. You should hesitate before celebrating, after all last year's profit could have been twenty-seven cents and this year's thirty-nine cents (a 46% increase). However, "the firm's cumulative profits over two years were less than the cost of a cup of Starbucks coffee" (Wheelan, 2013, p. 29).

Perhaps referencing the price of coffee produced an anchoring effect (Kahneman, 2011)—information that was imbedded in the homeowner's mind when subsequently deciding whether to vote, and if so, whether to vote yes. Table 2.3 presents the 2017 polling results. Voters approved the proposal 714 Yes to 491 No, with Yes comprising 59 percent of the total votes, an 18.4 percent margin of victory.[4]

POSTMORTEM ANALYSIS

Sticker Shock?

Prior to voting, the projected serial millage rates required to pay off the debt of the 2017 proposal were not widely disseminated. Column [B] of table 2.4 shows the millage rate schedule for retiring the District's *existing* debt at the time of the 2017 referendum. If the 2017 proposal had failed, and barring any future millage increase, the District's debt millage rate would decline to zero in 2030. However, it is likely at some point the Board would ask voters to approve a millage renewal rather than have its debt millage go to zero—requesting a millage renewal would probably have a better chance of voter approval than requesting new millage at some point beyond 2030.

Column [C] shows the projected additional millage if the 2017 proposal passed. Notice the much-publicized 0.75 rate was projected for each of the first nine years of the debt repayment. The projected additional rate exceeded 0.75 in each of the remaining sixteen years; from 2026–2041 the projected rates averaged 3.48, or 4.64 times the 0.75 rate. The average of Column [C] is 2.49, and when rounded, is the average annual 2.5 mills stated on the 2017 ballot. Column [C] data are plotted in figure 2.1.

Column [D] shows the projected total millage faced by homeowners if the proposal were approved. While the 9.64 rate depicted in each of the fifteen years spanning 2017–2031 was stated on the 2017 ballot, it was not an indicator of the projected annual millage *increase* over the twenty-five-year life of the bonds. Entering the single millage rate of 0.75 and the average homestead taxable value of $71,250 into the District's aforementioned calculator yielded a static estimate of $4.45 "for the monthly price of two cups of coffee."

Moreover, the bond payment schedule assumed the District's taxable value of property would increase 2.57 percent from 2017–2021 followed by 3 percent annual growth through 2041. Column [E] reveals these projected taxable values. Column [F] reports the projected twenty-five annual tax payments for the average homeowner with a 2017 taxable value of $71,250. The projected additional average annual tax payment was $271.56, yielding an average monthly payment of $22.63—the projected monthly price of two cups of coffee over twenty-five years. Instead of referring to a cup of Starbucks Unicorn Frappuccino, an $11 cup of coffee from the high-end Starbucks Reserve Roastery would have been a more accurate message.

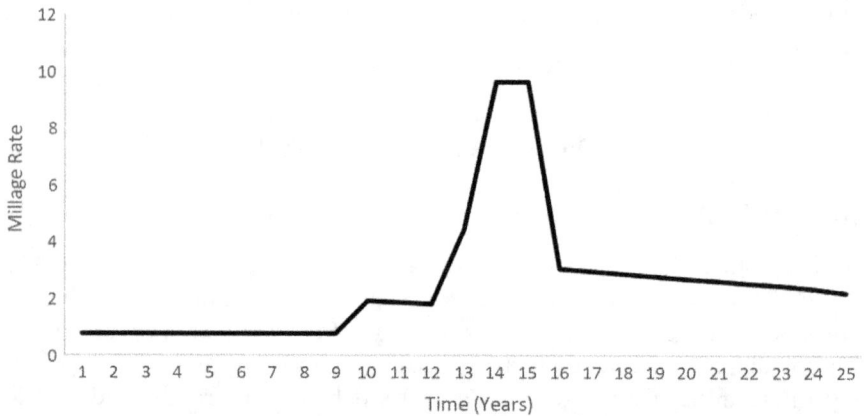

Figure 2.1 Projected Additional Millage Rates from Approval of 2017 Bond Proposal.

We have no idea how many registered voters (i) read and understood the District's web page or the bond payment schedule, (ii) used the tax calculator, (iii) viewed the Committee's web page or Facebook posting, (iv) were swayed by the Committee's postcard, phone calls, and personal contacts, or (v) read and understood the 2017 ballot. However, excerpts from two April 24, 2017, letters to the *DMG* suggest that the information in table 2.4 may not have been widely understood.

Table 2.4 Cost Ramifications of 2017 Bond Proposal

[A] Year	[B] Millage for Pre-2017 Debt	[C] Additional Millage if 2017 Proposal Passed	[D] Total Debt Millage if 2017 Proposal Passed	[E] Projected Growth of the 2017 Average Homeowner's Taxable Value^ ($)	[F] Projected Additional Taxes Paid ($) = [C]*[E]/1,000
2017	8.89	0.75	9.64	71,250	53.44
2018	8.89	0.75	9.64	73,081.13	54.81
2019	8.89	0.75	9.64	74,959.31	56.22
2020	8.89	0.75	9.64	76,885.76	57.66
2021	8.89	0.75	9.64	78,861.73	59.15
2022	8.89	0.75	9.64	81,227.58	60.92
2023	8.89	0.75	9.64	83,664.41	62.75
2024	8.89	0.75	9.64	86,174.34	64.63
2025	8.89	0.75	9.64	88,759.57	66.57
2026	7.74	1.90	9.64	91,422.36	173.70
2027	7.79	1.85	9.64	94,165.03	174.21
2028	7.85	1.79	9.64	96,989.98	173.61
2029	5.21	4.43	9.64	99,899.68	442.56
2030	0	9.64	9.64	102,896.67	991.92
2031	0	9.64	9.64	105,983.57	1,021.68
2032	0	3.04	3.04	109,163.08	331.86
2033	0	2.95	2.95	112,437.97	331.69
2034	0	2.86	2.86	115,811.11	331.22
2035	0	2.77	2.77	119,285.44	330.42
2036	0	2.68	2.68	122,864.00	329.28
2037	0	2.60	2.60	126,549.92	329.03
2038	0	2.52	2.52	130,346.42	328.47
2039	0	2.44	2.44	134,256.81	327.59
2040	0	2.34	2.34	138,284.52	323.59
2041	0	2.19	2.19	142,433.05	311.93
Average	4.34	2.49	6.83	—	271.56
Total					6,788.90

Source: Columns [A] through [D] are taken from the Schedule of Projected Millage Required to Repay Bonded Debt prepared for the Houghton-Portage Township Schools by the PFM group, financial and investment advisors, Ann Arbor, Michigan (undated). Schedule provided to the authors by the Houghton-Portage Township School District. Complete schedule available from the authors upon request. ^ Calculated assuming 2.57 percent annual growth from 2017–2021 followed by 3 percent annual growth through 2041.

- "Like many school districts across the UP [Upper Peninsula], the HPTS has proposed a .75 mill bond to make necessary improvements to the district's facilities."—S. D.
- "If your home's market value is $100,000 you will pay $37.50 per year for 25 years; a market value of $200,000 will pay two times as much: $75 per year; a market value of $300,000 three times: $112.50 per year etc. These payments will increase by approximately 1-2 percent per year as the assessed value of your property increases."—G. F.

Both writers mistakenly implied that the 0.75 millage rate would be levied annually in order to make the necessary payments to retire the additional debt. Even a local radio station, *The Wolf* 97.7, communicated the same precise, but inaccurate, message: "The bond would be paid by levying a millage of .75 mills for a maximum of 25 years" (Keweenaw Report, 2017). It is likely that other registered voters mistakenly believed that the projected additional millage was 0.75 annually over twenty-five years. Perhaps the 2017 ballot language resulted in *some* registered voters believing that the projected additional millage was 2.5 annually over twenty-five years. Of course, neither belief would have been accurate.

To the best of our knowledge, neither the information conveyed in table 2.4 nor the imagery of figure 2.1 was widely disseminated. Perhaps there was unwillingness for doing so due to a fear of inflicting sticker shock on the "average" homeowner upon learning of the proposal's projected tax increases due to the bond proposal—especially $991 and $1,021 looming in 2030 and 2031, respectively. Studies have shown that "voters may have 'sticker shock' if the bond calls for a large increase in taxes. Voters instead tend to favor 'neutral' taxation, which extends current taxes if one bond is paid off, and is seen as an acceptable way to fund needed facilities" (Florence, 2014, p. 14).

Here is an alternate framing of the issue. Suppose someone offered you a purchase agreement calling for you, the buyer, to receive deliverables. You knew the agreement required you to make twenty-five annual payments. Would you sign the agreement if you knew only the amount of the first-year payment, $53? Would you sign if you knew only the amount of the first-year payment and the average of the twenty-five annual payments, $271? Of course, if you knew the average over twenty-five years, you could calculate the sum of all the payments ($6,775). Would you then be willing to sign the agreement? Alternatively, lacking information about the variation in the annual payments, would (should) you refrain from signing?

In summary, 0.75 was the lowest projected additional millage rate over the life of the bonds. The twenty-five-year average of the projected additional rates was 2.5, or 3.33 times the widely "advertised" 0.75 rate. The highest projected additional rate of 9.64 was almost thirteen times the advertised rate. Thus, the Board and Committee's reductionist message of "0.75 mills requested—which will cost the average household about $4.45 each month"—was precise, but inaccurate, due to the absence of the projected serial costs from the storyline.

Descriptive Statistics

The 2017 tally of 1,205 voters was an 80 percent increase over 2016. More voters resulted in the turnout rate increasing by 72 percent (see table 2.3). A study of nearly 800 Michigan school bond referenda by Bowers, Metzger, and Militello (2010) found that, other factors held constant, the higher the turnout rate, the lower the chances of passing. Gong and Rogers (2014) examined some 600 Oklahoma school bond referenda:

> Higher-than-expected turnout is associated with lower bond approval shares and lower chances of passing. If school campaign efforts influence turnout decisions of marginal (non-habitual) voters, strategies may impact bond election outcomes. Results suggest that increased campaign spending efforts should target supportive voters rather than the general population. (p. 260)

Given the District's record of successful bond referendums (table 2.2), perhaps the failure of the 2016 referendum was due mostly to apathy on the part of supportive, but nonvoting, homeowners. If so, leading up to the 2017 referendum, one might have assumed that a sufficient number of yes voters would most likely vote in order to avoid back-to-back failures. Campaigning by the Board and Committee would be superfluous. Of course, this is speculation.

What is known is that actions by the Board and the Committee indicate that their members were unwilling to sit by idly gambling that, absent any prompting, the turnout of supportive homeowners would lead to success in 2017. This now appears to have been a good choice. Although there was no organized opposition to the 2017 proposal, the number of No votes increased by 45 percent (table 2.3). The 2017 public relations campaign conducted by Board and Committee members to get yes voters to vote most likely contributed to the 116 percent increase in Yes votes (table 2.3).

The incidence of homeownership could also affect the voting outcome. We obtained the official polling lists containing names and addresses of the District's 2016 and 2017 voters. We also obtained 2017 city and township property tax lists providing homeowner names, addresses, and taxable values of voters' homestead properties. Of course, some District residents not owning residential property voted. Since the public relations campaign focused on the cost confronting homeowners, we purged the 2016 and 2017 voters who were not residential property owners. The majority of purged voters were senior citizens residing in rental housing; the remainder were non-senior renters and individuals living in owner-occupied housing that they were not the owner. Table 2.5 reports the census of purged and homeowner voters. Homeowners comprised 83.4 percent and 84.8 percent of the voters in 2016 and 2017, respectively.

Table 2.5 also reports the total number of 2016 and 2017 voters (1,581), the number of voters voting on both proposals (473), and voting only in one of the referendums (635). Thus, a Venn diagram of voter counts would display 85 voters voting only in 2016, 550 voters voting only in 2017 and 473 voters voting in both years. The census of homeowner voters in 2016 and 2017 was 558 and 1,023, respectively.

Table 2.6 presents descriptive statistics for each of the two populations of homeowner voters. In each case, the mean taxable value exceeded the median taxable value—the data are positively skewed, with the mean taxable value being lower in 2017 ($72,967) than in 2016 ($73,129). Table 2.6 also reports the percentage of homeowner voters born prior to 1958. Evidence indicates a high concentration of *long-standing* elderly within a district has a strong and positive impact on school expenditures, while a high concentration of newly arriving elderly has a strong negative impact on expenditures (Berkman & Plutzer, 2004). It might be true that elderly voters helped to increase the yes vote count in one or both of the proposals. However, there was a higher percentage of elderly homeowner voters in 2016 compared to 2017,

Table 2.5 Census of Purged and Homeowner Voters

Municipality and Year	Number of Voters	Number and Percentage of Purged Voters	Number and Percentage of Voters Who Were Homeowners
2016			
City	406	74 (18.2)^	332 (82.0)
Township	263	37 (14.0)	226 (86)
Total	669	111 (16.6)	558 (83.4)
2017			
City	677	119 (17.6)	558 (82.4)
Township	528	63 (12.0)	465 (88)
Total	1,205	182 (15.0)	1,023 (85.0)
Total Number of 2016 and 2017 Voters			1,581
Number of Individuals Voting in 2016 *and* 2017			473
Number of Individuals Voting in 2016 *or* 2017			635

^Values in parentheses are percentages.

Table 2.6 Descriptive Statistics 2016 and 2107 Homeowner Voters

Taxable Value of Homestead ($)	
Part A: 2016 City and Township, n = 558	
Mode	26,083
Median	64,051
Mean	73,129
Maximum	241,917
Minimum	9,494
Standard Deviation	42,153
% of n with Taxable Value > $71, 250	42.8
% of n born prior to 1958	55.7
Part B: 2017 City and Township, n = 1,023	
Mode	23,802
Median	62,910
Mean	72,967
Maximum	292,827
Minimum	5,657
Standard Deviation	43,533
% of n with Taxable Value >$71, 250	42.7
% of n born prior to 1958	53.6

which runs counter to the idea that senior citizen homeowners clinched the 2017 yes vote.

The 2017 mean taxable value reported in table 2.6 ($72,967) is slightly above the $71,250 mean value reported in exhibit 1. Assuming a taxable value of $72,967, the bond schedule's projected average annual tax payment is $278, or an average monthly price of $23.17 for two cups of Starbucks Reserve Roastery coffee.

CONCLUSION

This study focused on cost information communicated during a 2017 school bond campaign. Public relations by its very nature can be subjective in advocating for a client or cause to influence thoughts or behaviors of publics. The campaign's precise language—"Proposed 0.75 Mills to support a $10.9 Million Bond Proposal"—and imagery—"for the price of about 2 cups of coffee a month"—were found to be not entirely accurate, but no doubt contributed to the success of the referendum. Keeping the projected serial millage rates and tax payments under the radar probably lowered the likelihood of widespread sticker shock among voters.

Sharing a wealth of cost information ran the risk of creating a wealth of confusion and a poverty of attention among homeowners.[5] The balancing act of sharing too much or too little information can be difficult. Explaining information to diverse publics can be even more difficult. Board and Committee members are to be applauded for tackling these difficulties for worthy intentions. In similar cases, boards and internal activists should seek the guidance of a public relations practitioner well versed in distilling and communicating complicated information. The National School Public Relations Association (NSPRA) Code of Ethics (adopted 1981) states in part:

> The education public relations professional shall be guided constantly by pursuit of the public interest through truth, *accuracy*, good taste and fairness; follow good judgment in releasing information; *not intentionally disseminate misinformation* or confidential data; avoid actions which lessen personal, professional or organizational reputation. [Italics added]

We surmise the Board and Citizens' Committee publicized the 2017 referendum in what they viewed as the best possible manner for securing a yes vote. We caution the reader from necessarily viewing the inaccuracy described in this study as being intentionally disseminated misinformation. The lesson learned from this study is that, in school bond referendums, avoiding the inaccuracy described here will likely diminish the possibility of publics suspecting the school board, school administrators, and internal activists of intentionally disseminating misinformation, thereby increasing the likelihood of a success in future campaigns.

EXHIBIT 4. 2016 AND 2017 BALLOTS

HOUGHTON-PORTAGE TOWNSHIP SCHOOL DISTRICT BONDING PROPOSAL

Shall Houghton-Portage Township School District, Houghton County, Michigan, borrow the sum of not to exceed Eight Million Six Hundred Ninety Thousand Dollars ($8,690,000) and issue its general obligation unlimited tax bonds therefor, for the purpose of:

remodeling, equipping and re-equipping and furnishing and re-furnishing school buildings; erecting, furnishing and equipping a press box and a concession stand addition to the fieldhouse; and preparing, developing, improving and equipping play fields, athletic fields and facilities and sites?

The following is for informational purposes only:

The estimated millage that will be levied for the proposed bonds in 2016, under current law is 1.71 mills ($1.71 on each $1,000 of taxable valuation) for a 1.38 mills net increase over the prior year's levy. The maximum number of years the bonds may be outstanding, exclusive of any refunding, is twenty-five (25) years. The estimated simple average annual millage anticipated to be required to retire this bond debt is 2.01 mills ($2.01 on each $1,000 of taxable valuation).

The school district expects to borrow from the State School Bond Qualification and Loan Program to pay debt service on these bonds. The estimated total principal amount of that borrowing is $2,274,538 and the estimated total interest to be paid thereon is $908,575. The estimated duration of the millage levy associated with that borrowing is 15 years and the estimated computed millage rate for such levy is 10.27 mills. The estimated computed millage rate may change based on changes in certain circumstances.

The total amount of qualified bonds currently outstanding is $14,355,000. The total amount of qualified loans currently outstanding is approximately $9,777,070.

(Pursuant to State law, expenditure of bond proceeds must be audited, and the proceeds cannot be used for repair or maintenance costs, teacher, administrator or employee salaries, or other operating expenses.)

YES ◉
NO ◉

HOUGHTON-PORTAGE TOWNSHIP SCHOOL DISTRICT BONDING PROPOSAL

Shall Houghton-Portage Township School District, Houghton County, Michigan, borrow the sum of not to exceed Ten Million Eight Hundred Ninety-Five Thousand Dollars ($10,895,000) and issue its general obligation unlimited tax bonds therefor, for the purpose of:

remodeling, equipping and re-equipping, and furnishing and refurnishing school buildings; erecting an exit canopy for the elementary school and a concession building and new bleacher system with press box for the middle/high school; acquiring, installing and equipping or re-equipping the middle/high school building for instructional technology; and preparing, developing, and improving athletic structures, athletic fields, and sites, including a new elementary school pickup/drop-off driveway?

The following is for informational purposes only:

The estimated millage that will be levied for the proposed bonds in 2017, under current law, is .75 mill ($0.75 on each $1,000 of taxable valuation). The maximum number of years the bonds may be outstanding, exclusive of any refunding, is twenty-five (25) years. The estimated simple average annual millage anticipated to be required to retire this bond debt is 2.50 mills ($2.50 on each $1,000 of taxable valuation).

The school district expects to borrow from the State School Bond Qualification and Loan Program to pay debt service on these bonds. The estimated total principal amount of that borrowing is $2,914,625 and the estimated total interest to be paid thereon is $1,710,742. The estimated duration of the millage levy associated with that borrowing is 15 years and the estimated computed millage rate for such levy is 9.64 mills. The estimated computed millage rate may change based on changes in certain circumstances.

The total amount of qualified bonds currently outstanding is $22,565,000. The total amount of qualified loans currently outstanding is approximately $138,555.

(Pursuant to State law, expenditure of bond proceeds must be audited, and the proceeds cannot be used for repair or maintenance costs, teacher, administrator or employee salaries, or other operating expenses.)

YES ○
NO ○

NOTES

1. Conventional school districts obtain funding for capital projects by establishing a sinking fund or borrowing money. Capital projects include purchasing land, constructing buildings, improving existing buildings, and adding new amenities and infrastructure.

A sinking fund acts as a savings account. Voters approve local property tax increases with the additional revenue earmarked for specific projects. Funds are withdrawn from the account to pay invoices for completed projects. Borrowing occurs when a district sells bonds. The state places limits on how much a district can borrow without gaining approval through a bond referendum. Districts seek voter approval to issue "qualified" or "nonqualified bonds." Qualified bonds are backed by the state's credit rating and its guarantee to pay back the loan if the district fails to do so. This guarantee usually results in a district borrowing at lower interest rates.

A district may borrow from the state an amount sufficient to enable the district to pay principal and interest requirements on its outstanding qualified bonds. Voter approval of the borrowing results in the school district's property taxes increasing to pay off the principal and interest necessary to "retire" the bonds. For more details, see Michigan Department of Treasury (2015).

2. The Michigan tax credit refunds property taxes paid by homeowners by reducing their state income tax payment. In 2017, to qualify for the credit the taxable value of the homeowner's home and their total household resources had to be less than $135,000 and $50,000, respectively (Michigan Department of Treasury, 2018b). Latest available figures (2014) show that, in the Houghton-Portage Township School District, 543 property tax credits were claimed totaling $213,358 or $393 on average (Michigan Department of Treasury, 2016).

3. The text at the bottom of exhibit 2 Part B says the estimated tax increase is lower if the homeowner took the property tax deduction when itemizing on his or her federal income tax return. Doing so does not change the fact that, the calculator's estimated annual tax bill increase was inaccurate due to the benign, but incorrect, assumption that the 0.75 millage rate would apply in each year that payments were made to retire the increased debt.

4. The District's referendum was among the fifty-five statewide qualified proposals in 2017, of which thirty-one (53%) passed. Among those fifty-five were nine that failed in 2016. Four of the nine sought more dollars and two were successful. The five remaining repeats sought less dollars and four were successful (Michigan Department of Treasury, 2018a).

5. Credit is due Nobel Laureate Herbert A. Simon: "A wealth of information creates a poverty of attention" (Excellent Journey, 2015).

REFERENCES

Berkman, M. B., & Plutzer, E. (2004). Gray peril or loyal support? The effects of the elderly on educational expenditures. *Social Science Quarterly*, *85*(5), 1178–1192.

Bowers, A. J., Metzger, S. A., & Militello, M. (2010). Knowing what matters: An expanded study of school bond elections in Michigan, 1998–2006. *Journal of Education Finance*, *35*(4), 374–396, doi:10.1353/jef.0.0024.

Cheng, E. (2017). The law of averages. *The Wall Street Journal*, July 15–16, C4.

Ciszek, E. L. (2015). Bridging the gap: Mapping the relationship between activism and public relations. *Public Relations Review*, *41*, 447–455.

City Data.com (2018). Retrieved from http://www.city-data.com/city/Houghton-Michigan.html.

Curtin, P. A. (2016). Exploring articulation in internal activism and public relations theory: A case study. *Journal of Public Relations Research*, *28*(1), 19–34, doi: 10.1080/1062726X.2015.1131696.

DeGrow, B. (2017). How school funding works in Michigan. Mackinac Center for Public Policy. Retrieved from https://www.mackinac.org/archives/2017/s2017-04.pdf.

Excellent Journey (2015). A poverty of attention. Retrieved from https://excellentjourney.net/2015/04/28/a-poverty-of-attention/.

Florence, L. L. (2014). School district bond campaigns: Strategies that ensure successful outcomes. Dissertations and Theses. Paper 1847. Retrieved from https://pdxscholar.library.pdx.edu/cgi/viewcontent.cgi?referer=&httpsredir=1&article=2847&context=open_access_etds.

Flynn, T. (2016). You had me at hello: How personal, developmental and socialcharacteristics influence communicator persuasiveness and effectiveness. *Research Journal of the Institute for Public Relations, 3*(1), 1–11. Retrieved from https://instituteforpr.org/wp-content/uploads/Terry-Flynn-2.pdf.

Gong, H., & Rogers, C. L. (2014). Does voter turnout influence school bond elections? *Southern Economic Journal, 81*(1), 247–262.

Hanover Research. (2012). Strategies to increase public support for bond measures. Retrieved from http://www.gssaweb.org/wp-content/uploads/2015/04/Strategies-to-Increase-Public-Support-for-Bond-Measures-1.pdf.

Holt, C. R. (2009). *School bond success: A strategy for building America's schools* (3rd ed.). New York: Rowman & Littlefield Education.

Holt, C. R., Wendt, M. A., & Smith, R. M. (2006). School bond success: An exploratory case study. *The Rural Educator*, Winter, 11–18.

Houghton Portage Township School District (2017). Homestead Property Tax Credit Model. Retrieved from http://www.pfmtaxcalc.com/houghtonportage/default.aspx.

Kahneman, D. (2011). *Thinking, fast and slow*. New York: Farrar, Straus and Giroux.

Keweenaw Report (2017). Bond proposal on may ballot for Houghton-Portage Township Schools. Retrieved from http://www.keweenawreport.com/news/local-news/bond-proposal-may-ballot-houghton-portage-township-schools/.

Levitin, D. J., (2016). *A field guide to lies*. New York: Dutton.

Michigan Department of Education (2018). Fast facts 2017–18: Statistics for Michigan Schools. Retrieved from https://www.michigan.gov/documents/mde/MDE_Fast_Fact_379573_7.pdf.

Michigan Department of Treasury (2015). Bureau of state and authority finance school bond qualification and loan program annual report. Retrieved from https://www.michigan.gov/documents/treasury/SBQLPAnnualReport_456025_7.pdf.

Michigan Department of Treasury (2016). Michigan income, income tax, and property tax credits by school district 2014. Retrieved from http://www.michigan.gov/documents/treasury/IIT_and_HPTC_by_sd_by_2014_ADA_passed_565103_7.pdf.

Michigan Department of Treasury (2018a). School elections for state qualified bonds 1996–present. Retrieved from https://treas-secure.state.mi.us/apps/findschoolbondelectinfo.asp.

Michigan Department of Treasury (2018b). Michigan Taxes. Retrieved from https://www.michigan.gov/taxes/0,4676,7-238-43535_43538-155081--,00.html.

Michigan State University Extension (2014). Reading your property assessment notice. Retrieved from http://msue.anr.msu.edu/news/reading_your_property_assessment_notice.

National School Public Relations Association Code of Ethics (adopted 1981). Retrieved from https://www.nspra.org/code-ethics.

Savary, J., Goldsmith, K., & Dhar, R. (2015). Giving against the odds: When tempting alternatives increase willingness to donate. *Journal of Marketing Research, LII*, 27–38.

Wheelan, C. (2013). *Naked statistics: Stripping the dread from the data.* New York: W. W. Norton.

Chapter 3

The Importance of Shared Vision and Stakeholder Influence on K-12 School Leaders' Efforts to Improve Student Mathematics Achievement

Emma P. Bullock and Patricia S. Moyer-Packenham

> *In **human relations**, this is obvious: I* never *react to you but to **you-plus-me**; or to be more accurate, it is **I-plus-you** reacting to **you-plus-me**. "I" can never* influence *"you" because you have* already influenced me; *that is, in the very process of meeting, by the very process of meeting, we BOTH become something **different**. It is I plus **the-interweaving-between-you-and-me** meeting you plus **the-interweaving-between-you-and-me**, etc., etc. If we were doing it mathematically we would work it out to the* nth *power.*
>
> (Follett, 1924, pp. 62–63; Graham, 1995, p. 42; Jörg, 2016, p. 72)

School leaders are often tasked with improving student mathematics achievement, as measured by standardized assessments (Bottoms & Schmidt-Davis, 2010; Schmidt-Davis & Bottoms, 2012). When improvements do not happen quickly enough, solutions can involve changes in school leadership (Heissel & Ladd, 2017; McAlister, 2013; Player & Katz, 2016; Strunk, Marsh, Hashim, Bush-Mecenas, & Weinstein, 2016). However, school leaders do not operate in a proverbial vacuum.

Many factors play into school improvement efforts, and without understanding the complexity of the problem, often solutions are inadequate leading to disappointed efforts, huge expenditures of funds, and frustrated communities (Dillon, 2011). Complexity Theory provides a way in which to model schools as complex adaptive systems (CASs), considering the many moving parts and intricacies that exist in real-life scenarios.

To help school leaders who may be confronted with this complex phenomenon, the purpose of this article is to describe, through the lens of Complexity Theory, the influences of various stakeholders on school leaders and examine the associated differences in school leaders' efforts to improve student mathematics achievement outcomes.

LITERATURE REVIEW

Complexity Theory Applied to School Organizations

The word "complexity" originally was a noun, meaning objects with many interconnected parts (Holland, 2014). Today complexity designates a diverse scientific field that studies complex systems across many disciplines and settings. There are many ways to think about systems. One definition of a system is "an assemblage or combination of things or parts forming a complex or unitary whole" ("System [Def. 1]," 2015). However, a complex system demonstrates an additional distinctive property called emergence.

Emergence is a form of collaboration in which the collective actions of the complex system in its entirety are more than the sum of the actions of its parts. Because of this, an emergent property is nonlinear and can be difficult to define operationally. An example of an emergent property would be the "school culture" associated with an aggregate of stakeholders (i.e., students, parents, teachers, and school leaders) in an educational institution (hereafter referred to as a school). It is impossible to define a "school culture" based on one individual stakeholder. It is only when the stakeholders work in aggregate that school culture emerges and is perceived as a property of a school.

This nonlinearity of emergent properties leads to the necessity of hierarchical levels of organization in order to define the properties themselves. For example, without the lower level of the stakeholders in aggregate, it becomes futile to define "school culture." It is only at the higher hierarchical level of organization, found when stakeholders combine to become a school, that the property of school culture emerges. Thus, Complexity Theory attempts to describe the challenges associated with understanding complex systems, their emergent properties, and hierarchical levels of organization with the purpose to attain some ability to guide the complex system toward some desired end.

A CAS has individual elements of the system that are not fixed. In other words, these individual elements can learn and adapt in response to interactions with other elements of the complex system. The literature usually refers to these elements as agents (Holland, 2014; Jäppinen, 2014; Mason, 2008; Stanley, 2006).

Schools fit under the CAS classification due to the regular change in the individual agents of the complex system. This idea of elements of the complex system as agents contributes to the concept of agency (Davis, Phelps, & Wells, 2004). It is through the interactions of the individual agents, or agency, that complex emergence occurs. For the purposes of this study, we use the term stakeholders as a replacement for elements, or agents, since the CAS in question is a school.

Because individual stakeholders of a CAS, such as a school, are in a constant state of change (i.e., student mobility, faculty and staff movement, and levels of parental involvement), it is impossible to expect every stakeholder to converge upon a single "optimal" strategy for almost any decision-making process. As stakeholders interact with each other, adapt, and correspondingly change (e.g., utilize agency), new ideas about decision-making processes will usually emerge.

This type of complex feedback loop, in which the agency among stakeholders influences each other's decisions, makes CASs difficult to analyze or even describe (Gilstrap, 2005; Stanley, 2006). However, to treat a school as anything other than a CAS fails to recognize the contextual realities in which school leaders are placed (Koopmans & Stamovlasis, 2016).

Influence of Leadership

Several components are essential to the phenomena of leadership: (a) leadership is a process, (b) leadership involves influence, (c) leadership occurs in groups, and (d) leadership involves common goals (Northouse, 2016). Leadership is vital to the effectiveness of a school, and recent research has shown that school leadership affects student achievement (Malloy & Leithwood, 2017; Shatzer, Caldarella, Hallam, & Brown, 2014; Tan, 2018).

For example, Leithwood, Louis, Anderson, and Wahlstrom (2004) concluded that the school leader was second only to the classroom teacher among school-related factors affecting school achievement, with a quarter of the school effects on student achievement attributed to the direct and indirect effects of the school leader. Likewise, Marzano and colleagues' (2005) meta-analysis of thirty-five years of research indicated that school leadership has a substantial effect on student achievement. With this study, we sought to better understand the phenomenon of school leadership specifically with respect to student mathematics achievement.

Analyzing Influences through the Lens of Complexity Theory

Currently, there is limited empirical research applying Complexity Theory to school leadership at the level of the school as an organization. Empirical studies utilizing Complexity Theory in educational settings have only been found in recent publications. In the past few years, Complexity Theory has been used to investigate daily high school attendance data (Koopmans, 2016), identify nonlinear dynamical interaction patterns in collaborative groups (Stamovlasis, 2016), investigate teacher-student interactions (Pennings & Mainhard, 2016), and study the effectiveness of a science and technology educational intervention (van Vondel, Steenbeck, van Dijk, & van Geert, 2016).

Bower (2006) conducted a qualitative phenomenological study that examined the experiences of the faculty of one middle school through the lens of Complexity Theory to better understand the phenomena of self-organization and its role in sustaining school improvement. Bower framed the study by classifying sustained school improvement as an emergent property from within a school. He made this distinction due to the recognition that the core processes of principles, philosophy, and values (i.e., a shared vision) influenced processes such as feedback, communication, dialogue, sense making, and relationships leading to the emergent ownerships, renewal, creativity, safe and trusting atmosphere, engagement, and self-organization which are needed to make sustained improvement possible.

Bower found indirect influences of the school leader on individuals and collective groups of teachers to be important to sustain reform efforts and improvement. There was a continual feedback loop between the school leader's actions with staff, the concept of shared leadership, the collective actions of the faculty, and sustained results. Further results suggested the dynamics of self-organization needed collective leadership that focused on collective ownership to sustain improvements over time.

While not addressing Complexity Theory explicitly, Higgins and Bonne's (2011) two-year case study examined how and why four leadership functions were enacted in an elementary school with a particular focus on hierarchical and heterarchical configurations of leadership. They found that the influences felt between hierarchical and heterarchical levels strengthened the school's work toward sustaining reform efforts in promoting the teaching and achievement of mathematics. This investigation into the influences between different stakeholders acknowledged the complexities of school leadership and thus has application to the present inquiry.

In their books, while Davis and Sumara (2008) and Uhl-Bien and Marion (2008) discuss the theoretical applications to, and suggest methodological approaches for, the use of complexity to school leadership and educational research, the actual implementation of the ideas discussed is negligible to nonexistent. While McQuillan and Kershner (2018) applied these ideas in a recent case study of one successful urban school leader, conceptualizing the principal as a critical leverage point within the broader complex adaptive system of the school, this study seeks to fill this gap using a larger sample size representing many schools with differing demographics in order to see broader patterns of emergence.

Shared Vision

The concept of a shared vision has its roots in transformational leadership theory and research. Kouzes and Posner (1987, 2002) identify the concept of a shared vision as one of the five fundamental practices that empower leaders to achieve their goals. A shared vision occurs when leaders create a compelling perspective that inspires and guides stakeholder's behavior. This is done through a process of visualizing positive outcomes and communicating them effectively to other stakeholders (Johnson, 2013; Vale et al., 2010).

In a similar vein, the concepts of shared, or distributed leadership, emerge from the complexities of adaptive leadership and the creation of a shared vision. In the context of Complexity Theory, shared leadership occurs when stakeholders in a CAS take on leadership behaviors (agency) to influence and maximize the effectiveness of the whole (i.e., school; Northouse, 2016). Thus, stakeholders share influence in the creation of the shared vision.

CONCEPTUAL FRAMEWORK

The convergence of Complexity Theory and the influences of leadership give rise to the *School Leadership in a Complex Adaptive System (SL-CAS) Framework* (see figure 3.1).

The framework is unique; in that it recognizes an educational institution, or school, as a CAS (represented as a funnel; Gilstrap, 2005), containing internal units (i.e., groups of stakeholders such as teacher teams, parent organizations, and student demographics) of operating chaotic systems (represented as circles inside the funnel) in which both individual stakeholders and groups of stakeholders have agency (i.e., interactions with each other represented by two-way arrows between the circles; Bruner, 1996; Jörg, 2016). This agency leads to complex emergence in which new practices and customs emerge at higher hierarchical levels of organization (Davis et al., 2004).

Using the school leader as a lens (represented by the darker black two-way arrows and darker outlined circle), it then becomes a question of what role does school leaders' agency play in guiding the CAS toward the trajectory (i.e., the goal represented as the arrow in which the complex system is moving toward) to increase student mathematics achievement (Dewey, 1998; Eriksen & Cunliffe, 2010; Grotzer, 2012; Jordan, 2010; Jörg, 2011, 2016; Lincoln & Guba, 1985; McClellan, 2010; Mowat & Davis, 2010; Osberg, Biesta, & Cilliers, 2008; Vygotsky, 1978).

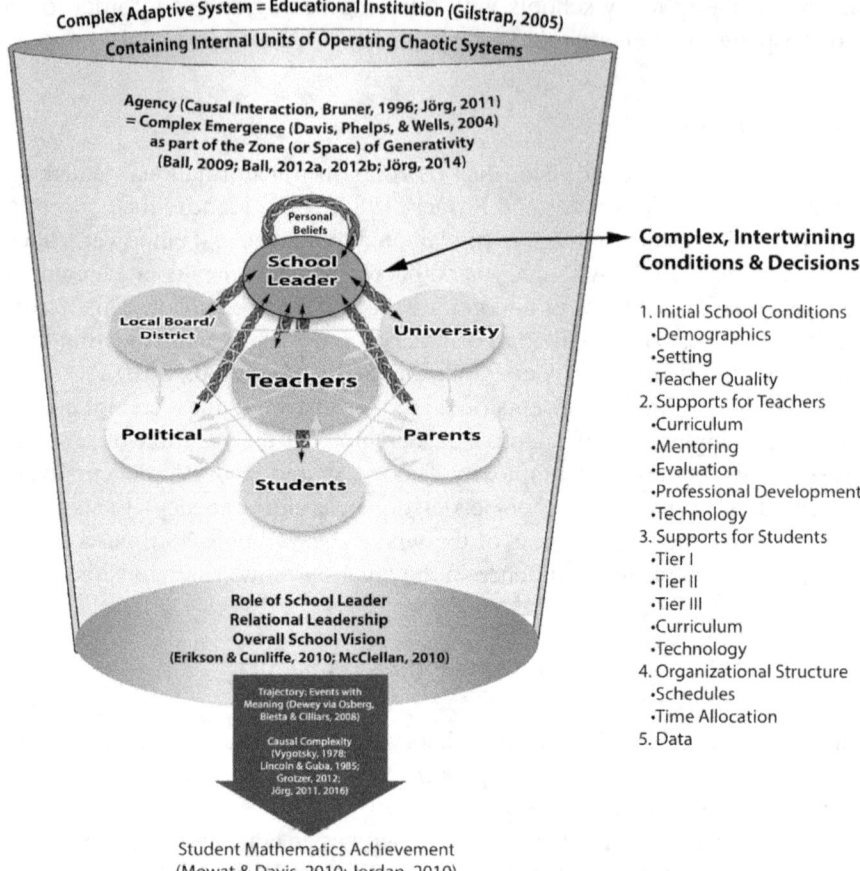

Figure 3.1 Conceptual Framework of School Leadership in a Complex Adaptive System (SL-CAS). This figure illustrates the dynamic organizational system known as a school with internal units of operating chaotic systems, complex feedback loops, and a school's trajectory with respect to student mathematics achievement emphasizing the role of the school leader.

At play is also the agency of various stakeholders with respect to initial school conditions, supports for teachers, supports for students, the organizational structure of the school, and the availability and use of data, which is represented by the complex braid twisting around the influences between various stakeholders. These impacts on the influences represented combine, weave together, and interact to affect the desired outcomes (Ball, 2009, 2012b, 2012a; Jörg, 2014) and must be considered to understand the influences on school leaders as they work to promote student mathematics achievement.

As an emerging construct, the school leadership in a CAS framework provides a means for analyzing and interpreting the complex realities of schools.

RESEARCH DESIGN

In an effort to provide help for school leaders engaged in the complex phenomenon of trying to improve student mathematic achievement, we employed a phenomenological qualitative research design (Creswell, 2013). In this type of design, the focus is on understanding what groups of individuals experience with respect to some commonly shared phenomenon by describing their perceptions and perspectives. In this way, we sought to discuss the essence of school leaders' experiences, as they acted with other stakeholders (i.e., teachers, parents, district offices, local school boards, legislative bodies, and students) to guide their CAS toward high student mathematics achievement and to interpret the meaning of these shared experiences.

Research Questions

The following research questions guided this study:

1. What types of stakeholder influences (i.e., teachers, students, parents, and school boards) do school leaders describe with respect to improving student mathematics achievement in their schools?
2. How do these influences then impact school leaders' decisions and actions with respect to improving student mathematics achievement in their schools?
3. How are these influences and subsequent decisions and actions of school leaders associated with student mathematics achievement at their schools?

Participants and Settings

Participants were selected using purposeful maximal variation sampling to identify sixteen school leaders, representing traditional public and charter schools in Utah. The reason for this sampling decision was to be able to describe the commonly lived experiences of school leaders trying to guide a CAS to improve student mathematics achievement through as many demographically diverse situations as possible; thus, capturing the complexity of the phenomena and allowing for a more complete interpretation of the results.

Sampling criteria included varying by student mathematics achievement (as measured by Utah's 2015 Student Assessment of Growth and Excellence (SAGE) standardized student test scores in mathematics), school settings (e.g., urban, suburban, or rural), and student demographics (e.g., percent low-SES, percent minority, percent SpEd).

School leaders were divided into three focus groups: five school leaders from schools performing higher than their demographics would suggest (referred to as "Higher"), six school leaders from schools performing about where their demographics would suggest (referred to as "As Expected"), and six school leaders from schools performing lower than their demographics would suggest (referred to as "Lower"), with one school leader representing rural schools in both the Higher and the As Expected groups (Collins, 2010) for a total of sixteen distinct participants.

School leaders were from schools demographically similar to others from their rankings (USOE Public Data Gateway website found at https://datagateway.schools.utah.gov/). This website defines twenty "similar" schools in a cohort as follows:

> **What are "similar schools"?** Similar schools are defined by using a statistical approach based on Polytopic Vector Analysis (PVA). In the 2015 edition, schools were analyzed using the size of the school (in terms of October 1 enrollment), percentages of the student population who are ethnic minority, low income, and English language learners, and two measures of rurality based on locale codes assigned by the U.S. Bureau of the Census.

Thus, twenty schools listed as a demographically similar cohort were analyzed. Each school was then assigned a ranking from one to twenty, based on SAGE mathematics proficiency scores, within the similar schools cohort. Thus, schools ranked from one to five out of the twenty were performing relatively Higher. Schools ranked from six to fifteen were performing As Expected. Schools ranked from sixteen to twenty were performing relatively Lower.

Table 3.1 shows the variation of school demographics represented by each school leader focus group. The five school leaders from schools performing Higher represented three suburban, one rural, and one urban school. They also represented four traditional public and one K-12 charter school (comprising a total of three elementary and two secondary schools). The six school leaders from schools performing As Expected represented three suburban, two rural, and one urban school. They also represented five traditional public and one charter school and three elementary and three secondary schools.

The six school leaders from schools performing Lower represented one suburban, three rural, and two urban schools. They also represented three

Table 3.1 School Demographics Represented by Focus Group Participants' School Performance

School Performance	Enrollment (N)	Ethnic Minority(%)	Low Socioeconomic Status (%)	English Language Learners (%)	Special Education (%)
Higher	75–1,373	2.7–64.7	11.4–82.7	0–42.3	0.2–13.7
As Expected	122–1,616	6.4–47.4	6–80.3	0–23.6	10.7–21.3
Lower	67–692	10.4–79.4	19.9–99.7	0–72.9	9.9–14.3

Eth. Min stands for "Ethnic Minority", Low SES stands for "Low Socioeconomic Status", ELL stands for "English Language Learners", SpEd stands for "Special Education".

elementary and three secondary schools and four traditional public and two charter schools.

Data Collection

We collected video and audio data and used a semi-structured, focus group interview protocol to illicit spontaneous and genuine responses (Vaughn, Schumm, & Sinagub, 1996). The interview protocol was initially developed through the lens of Complexity Theory and based on the SL-CAS theoretical framework and was tested prior to the focus group interviews. There were seven focus group interviews with a total of sixteen participants that took place over a two-month period. Each interview occurred during one two-hour session. Five of the focus group interviews took place in a centrally located hotel conference room around a large table.

One focus group interview was conducted in a library study room, and one was conducted in a university conference room. Two of the focus groups included one or more participants participating via Skype or Google Hangouts. Three school leaders participated electronically. All others participated in person. To ensure the quality of participation was not impacted due to the difference of in-person versus electronic participation, the facilitators actively mediated the conversations to ensure equal participation. In addition, participants were assigned pseudonyms in order to ensure confidentiality.

Data Analysis

Traditional constant comparative analysis procedures utilizing the lens of Complexity Theory were employed. The interviews were transcribed and coded with three phases of coding: open, axial, and selective (Creswell, 2013) utilizing NVivo11 qualitative analysis software (Edhlund & McDougall, 2016). During the open coding phase, we reviewed the video recordings, audio recordings, transcripts, and field notes for salient categories of information until saturation was reached (Creswell, 2013).

The initial codes evolved around the SL-CAS theoretical framework and included such categories as: internal operating chaotic units (i.e., stakeholder groups); the influences of such groups on the school leader and vice versa; the presence, or lack thereof, of a shared vision; and decisions regarding resources, curriculum, time, mentoring and coaching, feedback, teacher professional development, and instructional methods.

Once we developed an initial set of categories, we used axial-coding categories to connect the open coding categories into overarching themes. Finally, selective coding was utilized to build a description, grounded in Complexity Theory, which connected the categories (Creswell, 2013) and answered the research questions.

RESULTS

School leaders were influenced in their decisions and actions, with respect to improving student mathematics achievement in their schools, by various stakeholder groups, depending on school performance. The results are organized into three sections that discuss the findings relevant to stakeholder groups that school leaders described as influencing their decisions and actions with respect to improving student mathematics achievement. The first section reports the findings for school leaders at schools performing Higher than their demographics would suggest. The second section reports the findings for school leaders at schools performing As Expected. The final section reports the findings for school leaders at schools performing Lower than expected.

Schools Performing Higher

Relative Strength of Stakeholder Influence Felt by the School Leader

Figure 3.2 shows the influences on school leaders, and vice versa, at schools whose school-wide mathematics proficiency scores were Higher than their demographics suggest. The red arrows indicate the influences felt on other stakeholders from the school leader or by the school leader from other stakeholders.

The black arrows indicate influences felt by the school leader on themselves. The thickness of the arrows indicates the relative strength of the influences as perceived and described by the school leaders who participated in the focus group interviews. The thickness of the arrows also indicates the identified frequency with which the influences were described by school leaders in comparison to other influences.

Figure 3.2 shows that the most influential stakeholders on school leader's decisions at schools performing Higher were generally teachers, the local

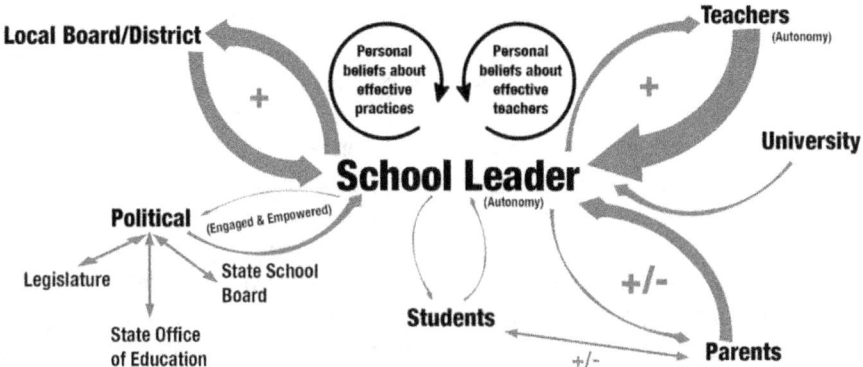

Figure 3.2 **Influences on Stakeholders and School Leaders in Schools Performing Higher than Their Demographics Would Suggest.** This figure illustrates the influences ranked from most influential to least influential as perceived by the school leader. The thicker the arrow, the more the school leader perceived its influence.

school board and/or district office, and parents, in that order. As Matt indicated, "By far the teachers are the most influential with me. I rely on them. . . . I trust my teachers." Nick agreed, "Definitely the teachers . . . they're the ones . . . in the trenches." However, Audra said, "I would say that the board is probably first . . . . My teachers would be the next . . . they are the ones that have the knowledge and the understanding of math." Jack concurred with Matt and Nick but included parental influences, "It's usually going to be . . . the teachers . . . [also] probably . . . parents."

In addition, school leaders described the interactions between teachers and school leaders and the local school board and/or district office primarily as positive in both directions. Finally, school leaders were strongly influenced by their own personal beliefs about effective practices and effective teachers, moderately influenced by university sources, and in a smaller way, influenced by students.

How Stakeholder Influences Impact School Leaders' Decisions and Actions to Improve Student Mathematics Achievement

In every case, school leaders in this group indicated a unified philosophy about effective instructional strategies between themselves and the teachers and the local school board and/or district office. With regard to this, Matt indicated that "the two . . . most powerful influences" were "this professional body which includes district math specialists and school based math teachers who have this philosophy of what math instruction should look like."

While Jack said, "I believe that the teachers were pretty free to choose how they taught the math. Some of the influences I guess that lead to that were some of the NCTM documents . . . the professional teaching standards." Charles stated, "It's interesting. The elementary, for a while, was the top elementary in the state. It's because I have four teachers there that have been there for 20 years together. . . . They know what it takes."

Combined with this unified philosophy about effective instructional strategies, school leaders consistently described a distributed ownership of data among various stakeholders and a distributed leadership style. Audra gave a detailed explanation of how these worked together in a recent scenario at her school where teachers "gave me three different proposals" and they implemented the first proposal. However, "when we tried that the first year, it didn't work." So, she described going back with the math teachers and looking at the plan again and going with the second proposal. She said, "The grades were much higher. We [felt] really happy with that."

School leaders at schools performing Higher indicated both positive and negative influences by parents, but not in an adversarial way. They viewed parents as partners in the educational effort of students. Audra indicated, "The parents want to have their students get through as much college as possible and so the parents are pushing their kids, sometimes."

Emergent Property of Shared Vision

Taken together, this provided evidence of an emergent property of a shared vision surrounding mathematics education as articulated by the school leader. Table 3.2 summarizes these common characteristics, or themes, among schools performing Higher than their demographics suggest.

Schools Performing As Expected

Relative Strength of Stakeholder Influence Felt by the School Leader

Figure 3.3 shows the influences on school leaders, and vice versa, in schools whose school-wide mathematics proficiency scores were As Expected based on their demographics.

In figure 3.3, the most influential stakeholders on school leader's decisions were political groups, particularly the state legislature and the state office of education. These were followed by the local school board and/or district office, teachers, and themselves, in that order. Political influences were particularly strong with this group. School leaders primarily expressed frustration with the state legislature and state office of education, with very little mention of the state school board.

Table 3.2 Schools Performing Higher: Shared Vision of Mathematics Education

Characteristics	Description
Unified philosophy about effective instructional strategies	School leaders indicated that teachers, school leaders, and the local school board/district office demonstrated a common understanding of effective instructional strategies with respect to mathematics education.
Distributed ownership of data	School leaders indicated that multiple stakeholder groups have regular and consistent access to student mathematics data. Furthermore, this data was routinely discussed and interpreted between stakeholder groups often without the direct facilitation of the school leader themselves.
Distributed leadership model	School leaders indicated that school-level decisions with respect to mathematics education were made in collective and cooperative ways, particularly with teachers and parents.
School leader autonomy	School leaders indicated they felt they had the ability to make school-level decisions with respect to mathematics education without undue interference from external influences.
Teacher autonomy	School leaders indicated that they felt that the teachers in their school had the ability to make classroom-level decisions with respect to mathematics education without undue interference from external influences.
Parents as partners	School leaders indicated a generally positive relationship with parents, in which parents and the school were working together for student success in mathematics education.

These expressions were characterized by a sense of helplessness and of being acted upon in negative ways without the ability to do anything about it. Candace said, "I . . . feel like the legislature/state office has that top ranking because they come up with the standards and that's where it all starts." Jay said, "I would say the highest would be the state level. The second would then be me, followed by local or the school board." Susan agreed:

> But also for me, it's external requirements. The core is the core and we aren't going to change the core for our single campus. I would say the higher-level influences decisions that support implementing resources that achieve the core, the standards.

School leaders perceived the interactions between teachers and school leaders and the local school board and/or district office in both positive and negative ways. Kay described a negative, "We [meaning school leaders] have

INFLUENCES ON SCHOOL LEADERS FOR SCHOOLS THAT ARE PERFORMING ABOUT WHERE THEIR DEMOGRAPHICS WOULD SUGGEST

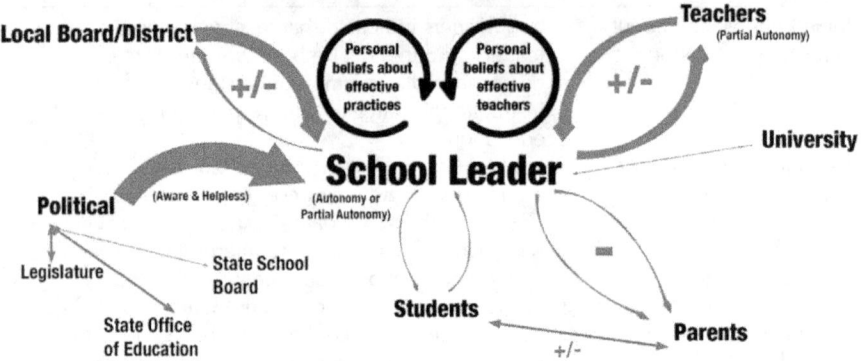

Figure 3.3 Influences on Stakeholders and School Leaders in Schools Performing As Expected by Their Demographics. This figure illustrates the influences ranked from most influential to least influential as perceived by the school leader. The thicker the arrow, the more the school leader perceived its influence.

very little input at all." Candace added a positive, "[The district] just finished writing the textbook for fourth, fifth, and sixth grade, rather than adopting one from a national company . . . ." School leaders were also influenced in a small way by students and slightly by university sources.

How Stakeholder Influences Impact School Leaders' Decisions and Actions to Improve Student Mathematics Achievement

School leaders in this group frequently referred to a non-unified philosophy about effective instructional strategies between themselves and the teachers and/or the local school board and/or district office. Most of these were disagreements between school leaders and one or more teachers at their school. Jay indicated disagreement with a teacher, "We've had one teacher, who for years has just really struggled, management and discipline as well as getting on the same page and working with some of those other teachers."

Dakota also indicated a similar disagreement, "We're still doing a lot of procedural things, especially in the younger grades." However, Kay indicated disagreement with her district, who advocated teaching multiple solution strategies:

> Everybody learns 3 or 4 different ways to solve the same kind of a problem, which is wonderful. But, really, do you want to do that to a second grader? . . . it's just very frustrating to me. . . . I think we need to just back off a bit and quit comparing ourselves to Singapore Math and everybody else, because it's not

apples with apples. You have to do this, and you have to memorize this, and you have to do this. That seems to help.

In addition to this non-unified philosophy about effective instructional strategies, school leaders consistently described a directive ownership of data. In this type of data ownership, school leaders described themselves as the primary holders of school data, and they determined how that data was distributed among other stakeholders. As such, school leaders described a more directive leadership style with various attempts to move toward a more distributive leadership style. Charles's statement was typical of what was said:

> Every time we sit down for a PLC, we look at their data and then we talk about it. If there's a particular area they're struggling in, or 70% of the kids in the class didn't do well, then definitely there's an issue there. Why is that? We pick it apart and then we just have conversations about what do you need and let's look at this data. It appears that something happened here, and I try to get them to figure out, because they usually know. "I taught it too fast, or I thought the kids knew more than they really did so now I have to go back and re-teach it," or whatever. Or maybe it's just a little handful of kids that 70% of the kids got it, but 30% didn't. Well, what are we going to do with that 30%?

In addition, school leaders primarily indicated negative influences by parents, often in adversarial terms. Thus, parents were often viewed as adversarial partners in the educational effort of students. One typical statement included this exchange:

Susan: If parents don't communicate to their children that persevering through solving math problems that don't come easy, is an important skill to develop, like exercising that muscle. If they just say, "Well it's too hard and I can't help you, this is dumb that you were even assigned this problem if you can't do it on your own," or whatever, if they send a message that they are themselves not good at math or they don't value math, it's harder for the kids to have the buy in.
Kay: I agree with that 100% 'cause I'll have a kid come back and say, "Well I can't do that. My mom couldn't do it either. She said she's always been bad at math. So, I'm bad at math, too." They look to it, sometimes I think as an excuse for why should I try?
Susan: Or like the parent who writes on the homework assignment, "I'm an engineer and I can't figure out what they're asking. This is dumb."
Kay: Yeah, that helps a lot.
Susan: I think the attitude of the parents definitely sways how willing the kids are to try or not try or complete homework or not.

Emergent Property of Disparate Vision

Taken together, this provides evidence of an emergent property of a disparate vision surrounding mathematics education as articulated by the school leader but with many expressions of trying to move toward a shared vision. Table 3.3 summarizes common characteristics among schools performing As Expected.

Table 3.3 Performing As Expected: Disparate Vision of Mathematics Education (Trying to Move toward a Shared Vision)

Characteristics	Description
Non-unified philosophy about effective instructional strategies	School leaders indicated that one or more individuals from the teachers and/or local school board/district office stakeholder groups demonstrated differing understandings, as compared to the school leader, of effective instructional strategies with respect to mathematics education.
Directive ownership of data	School leaders indicated that a few stakeholder groups, as determined by the school leader, have regular and consistent access to student mathematics data. Furthermore, this data was routinely discussed and interpreted between stakeholder groups but more often with the direct facilitation of the school leader themselves.
Directive leadership model/ attempting to move toward a distributed leadership model	School leaders indicated that school-level decisions with respect to mathematics education were made in more top to bottom ways, particularly with teachers and parents.
School leader autonomy or partial autonomy	School leaders indicated they felt they had autonomy or partial autonomy to make school-level decisions with respect to mathematics education without undue interference from external influences.
Teacher partial autonomy	School leaders indicated that they felt that the teachers in their school sometimes had the ability to make classroom-level decisions with respect to mathematics education without undue interference from external influences.
Parents as adversarial partners	School leaders indicated a generally negative relationship with parents, in which parents and the school were often not working together for student success in mathematics education.

INFLUENCES ON SCHOOL LEADERS FOR SCHOOLS THAT ARE PERFORMING LOWER THAN WHAT THEIR DEMOGRAPHICS WOULD SUGGEST

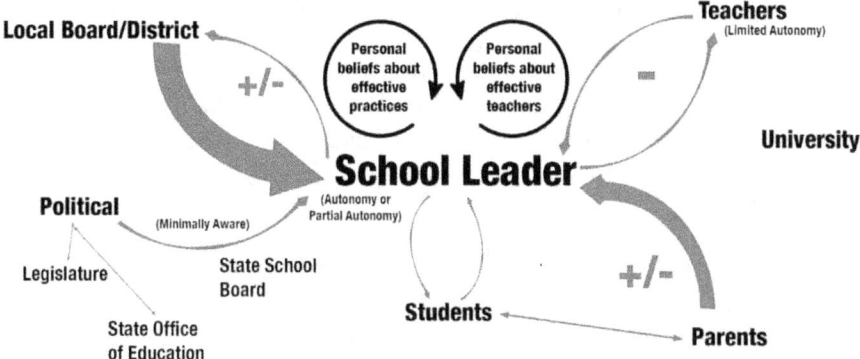

Figure 3.4 Influences on Stakeholders and School Leaders in Schools Performing Lower than Their Demographics Would Suggest. This figure illustrates the influences ranked from most influential to least influential as perceived by the school leader. The thicker the arrow, the more the school leader perceived its influence.

Schools Performing Lower

Relative Strength of Stakeholder Influence Felt by the School Leader

Figure 3.4 shows the influences on school leaders, and vice versa, in schools whose school-wide mathematics proficiency scores were Lower than what their demographics would suggest.

Figure 3.4 indicates that the most influential stakeholders on school leader's decisions were the local board and/or district office and parents, in that order. School leaders perceived the interactions between school leaders and the local school board and/or district office as both positive and negative, and these fell into two categories. Those who viewed this influence as primarily negative saw the local school board and/or district office as a sabotaging force or as lacking in support.

Grant gave such an example, "Our district is loud, especially with math, because they don't like that department." Kandy indicated, "We just lack support.... It doesn't exist.... It's like, 'Here you are! Teach!' It's very frustrating. It's frustrating for teachers. It's frustrating for me ... getting thrown into the position and not really knowing what I'm doing either." Those who saw this as a primarily positive influence viewed the local school board and/or district office as supportive, especially with respect to curriculum resources. Kelly said, "Probably the loudest voice we have is our district personnel for the math department and math curriculum department, because [our] district has created their own math program, K–6."

In addition, school leaders viewed parents both positively and negatively. Those who viewed parents positively perceived them as malleable and persuadable due to their total trust in what the school was doing. An example of this was discussed in this exchange between Arla and Judy:

Arla: Our parents don't feel empowered about school. . . . Our parents are almost all refugees and immigrants. . . . Culturally, they are not used to going to school and telling the school what to do. No parents are saying, "Oh you need to . . . ."
Judy: They're very trusting.
Arla: Very trusting and respectful.

Those who viewed parents negatively perceived them as unengaged, or as a sabotaging influence, such as Kandy who said:

Parent involvement, or the lack of . . . we don't have homework coming back . . . and they don't want their kids really to participate in things, because it takes them away from their jobs for one thing, and it takes them away from their family time, which is huge, really important . . . . So, they're not willing to participate.

School leaders in these groups did not describe parents as real partners in the educational process, although they wished this was different. School leaders were influenced in a small way by students and politics. None of the school leaders in this group even mentioned university influences.

How stakeholder influences impact school leaders' decisions and actions to improve student mathematics achievement. School leaders in this group frequently referred to an unknown or non-unified philosophy about effective instructional strategies between themselves and the teachers, while indicating that the teachers did not have a very influential voice at their schools. Judy was one school leader who viewed teachers as ineffective or unknowledgeable:

When I first got to my school, . . . I noticed that there was an inordinate amount of time in Tier II interventions, and not necessarily teachers running them. It was lots of staff pulling kids in and out. . . . So, we spent this last year really trying to get to the root cause of our academic failure. . . . We even went so far back as, "Here's what a standard is. Let's unpack it. What do kids need to be able to know, understand and do?" . . . I thought it would take us maybe a couple of months to get my teachers to the point where they were planning real explicit lesson plans that met the requirement of the standard and how they were going to assess them. It took us until March.

And, as with other school leaders in this group, Arla stated that her teachers "don't have that loud of a voice."

School leaders consistently described an underutilized directive ownership of data. In this type of data ownership, school leaders described themselves as the primary holders of school data; however, school leaders were often not able to quickly process or interpret the data in order to distribute it to other stakeholders in a timely way. In addition, school leaders in this group favored a more directive leadership style, with some minimal attempts to move toward a more distributive leadership style as evidenced from this statement by Kandy:

> [For] my presentation to the board, I made teachers write up strategies. This is what you're going to do to talk through the learning. There will be stations here. How are you going to build your time? What are you going to do with this block? They did that. Now it's just making sure that they're going to follow through on all these directions that they're going to use throughout the year. Anyway, hopefully it works.

Kelly also indicated this directive leadership style when referring to meetings he required teachers to attend to discuss various struggling student scenarios: "Because I knew some teachers would never come. . . . I made sure that everybody came." Judy shared similar sentiments as she referred to

Table 3.4 Schools Performing Lower: Disparate Vision of Mathematics Education (Minimal Attempts to Move toward a Shared Vision)

Characteristics	Description
Unknown or non-unified philosophy about effective instructional strategies	School leaders indicated that teachers, school leaders, and/or the local school board/district office did not demonstrate a common understanding of effective instructional strategies with respect to mathematics education.
Underutilized directive ownership of data	School leaders indicated that multiple stakeholder groups did not have regular and consistent access to student mathematics data. Furthermore, this data was not routinely discussed and interpreted between stakeholder groups without the direct facilitation of the school leader themselves.
Directive leadership model/minimal attempts to move toward a distributed leadership model	School leaders indicated that school-level decisions with respect to mathematics education are made top to bottom, particularly with teachers.
School leader autonomy or partial autonomy	School leaders indicated autonomy or partial autonomy to make school-level decisions with respect to mathematics education without undue interference from external influences.
Teacher limited autonomy	School leaders indicated that they felt that the teachers in their school did not have the ability to make classroom-level decisions with respect to mathematics education without interference from external influences.
Parents not partners	School leaders indicated a generally absent or sabotaging relationship with parents.

conversations with her teachers. "Then, you have to back up and say, 'Do you even know what your "I dos" should look like, because do you understand what the standard is requiring your students to be able to do?'"

Emergent Property of Disparate Vision

Taken together, this provides evidence of an emergent property of a disparate vision surrounding mathematics education as articulated by the school leader with some minimal expressions of trying to move toward a shared vision. Table 3.4 summarizes common characteristics among schools performing Lower than their demographics would suggest.

DISCUSSION

The purpose of this study was to describe the influences of stakeholders on school leaders and examine the school leaders' decisions and actions that impact student mathematics achievement while conceptualizing schools as CAS. The results showed that the types of influences described by school leaders on themselves, with respect to improving student mathematics achievement, differed based on school performance. This is consistent with SL-CAS framework which acknowledges the complex intertwining conditions that influence emergent decisions by the school leader.

For example, school leaders at schools performing Higher than expected described the teachers as the most influential stakeholders, followed by the local school board and/or district office and then parents. These relationships were mostly described as positive in nature with parents seen as partners. In addition, school leaders in Higher schools described an engaged and empowered relationship with political stakeholders such as the legislature, state office of education, and/or state school board and established relationships with university resources.

A shared vision of mathematics education emerged from the conversations as school leaders described a generally unified philosophy about effective instructional strategies, especially among teachers, administration, and the local school board/district office. Finally, these school leaders described a distributed leadership model and perceptions of school leader and teacher autonomy.

In contrast, school leaders in schools performing As Expected indicated that the most powerful influences on the school leader were political, followed by the local school board and/or district office, then teachers, then themselves. School leaders expressed frustration at their almost hyperawareness of external political influences while feeling helpless in the face of what they perceived as top-down decision-making.

In addition, district office/local school board relationships were characterized in both positive and negative ways with several expressing a loss of autonomy because of some negatively perceived influences. Furthermore, while school leaders in the As Expected schools depicted their relationships with teachers in both positive and negative ways, most descriptions were of good, high-quality teachers with a few exceptions.

In contrast to the school leaders in the Higher schools, school leaders in the As Expected schools described relationships with parents as adversarial. Often leaders described parental mindset as one of the most hindering influences on students' success. Unique to this group, school leaders indicated the importance of their own influence on themselves in their decision-making process.

In the cases of these CASs, a disparate vision of mathematics education (with school leaders trying to move their schools toward a shared vision) emerged from the conversations as school leaders described a non-unified philosophy about effective instructional strategies, especially between one or more of teachers, administration, and the local school board/district office. In addition, school leaders described a directive leadership model with attempts to move toward a distributed leadership model.

Finally, in schools performing Lower than expected, the local school board and/or district office was the most influential stakeholder on school leaders, followed by parents. School leaders described influences from these relationships as both positive and negative with a more top-down approach that left some feeling they had only partial autonomy in their decision-making. Again, school leaders described their relationships with parents both positively and negatively. Many expressed frustrations at the lack of parental involvement, such that parents were often not seen as partners in their students' mathematics success.

In contrast to the school leaders at schools performing Higher and As Expected, school leaders in Lower schools did not describe teachers as influential on the school leaders' decision-making. In the cases of these CASs, a disparate vision of mathematics education (with school leaders making minimal attempts to move their schools toward a shared vision) emerged from the conversations as school leaders described an unknown or non-unified philosophy about effective instructional strategies that was widespread.

This theme was especially found between administration and teachers. In addition, school leaders described a directive leadership model with minimal attempts to move toward a distributed leadership model and perception of teacher partial autonomy.

These differences in relational influences and patterns are clarified when viewed through the SL-CAS framework and shed light on the differences found in student mathematics achievement. The findings indicate that one reason schools may perform Higher than their demographics would suggest is due to the school-wide emergent property of a shared vision of mathematics education, which is evidenced by a unified philosophy about effective instructional strategies, especially between administrators, teachers, and the local school board and/or district office.

While the results do not indicate which came first, a shared vision also accompanies a distributed ownership of data and a distributed leadership model in conjunction with school leader and teacher autonomy and parental partnership. This provided further evidence of what Bower (2006) described as the phenomena of self-organization and its role in sustaining school improvement which is found in CAS. Indeed, this emergent self-organization of shared vision seems to be at the heart of school improvement as described by the school leaders in this study.

This result is also important as it confirms the research in line with transformational leadership theory in which shared vision is one of the five fundamental practices that empower leaders to achieve their goals (Kouzes & Posner, 1987, 2002). Johnson (2013) and Vale and colleagues' (2010) results indicate that a shared vision occurs when school leaders help facilitate a compelling prospect through a process of visualizing positive outcomes and effective communication with other stakeholders. The evidence from the school leaders at schools performing Higher than expected expressed the relational aspect of their leadership activity as described by Eriksen and Cunliffe's (2010) research.

They described collaboration activities in distributed leadership as the most import aspect of what helped students succeed in mathematics. The present research study adds to the body of literature in confirming the importance of cultivating an emergent property of a shared vision of mathematics education. This is particularly important to outperforming what would be expected by a school's demographics. Thus, modeling schools as CAS allows educational leaders to consider a pathway forward in navigating the complexities of their own school's initial conditions.

CONCLUSION

In conclusion, in conceptualizing schools as CAS, those whose students were able to perform higher in mathematics than their demographics would suggest displayed the emergent property of shared vision, as reported by school leaders, particularly between school leaders, teachers, and the district/local school board. The findings of this study support the research on shared vision generally (Alt, Díez-de-Castro, & Lloréns-Montes, 2015; Chorpita & Daleiden, 2014; Roueche, Baker III, & Rose, 2014; Strese, Keller, Flatten, & Brettel, 2016).

The findings also offer insight into understanding the influences of differing stakeholders as they may impact the self-organization necessary to move toward a shared vision of mathematics education within a school. By conceptualizing their schools through the lens of the SL-CAS framework, school leaders can be guided in their interactions with differing stakeholders to help facilitate their schools toward high student mathematics achievement.

REFERENCES

Alt, E., Díez-de-Castro, E. P., & Lloréns-Montes, F. J. (2015). Linking employee stakeholders to environmental performance: The role of proactive environmental strategies and shared vision. *Journal of Business Ethics*, *128*(1), 167–181. https://doi.org/10.1007/s10551-014-2095-x.

Ball, A. F. (2009). Toward a generative theory of change. *American Educational Research Review*, *46*(1), 45–72.

Ball, A. F. (2012a). *To know is not enough*. Presidential address presented at the AERA 2012 Annual Meeting, Vancouver, British Columbia, Canada. Retrieved from http://www.aera.net/Portals/38/docs/Annual_Meeting/Annual%20Meeting%20Theme%202012%20final.pdf.

Ball, A. F. (2012b). To know is not enough: Knowledge, power, and the zone of generativity. *Educational Researcher*, *41*(8), 283–293.

Bottoms, G., & Schmidt-Davis, J. (2010). *The three essentials: Improving schools requires district vision, district and state support, and principal leadership* (p. 64). Southern Regional Education Board (SREB).

Bower, D. F. (2006). Sustaining school improvement. *Complicity: An International Journal of Complexity and Education*, *3*(1), 61–72.

Bruner, J. (1996). *The culture of education*. Cambridge, MA: Harvard University Press.

Chorpita, B. F., & Daleiden, E. L. (2014). Structuring the collaboration of science and service in pursuit of a shared vision. *Journal of Clinical Child & Adolescent Psychology*, *43*(2), 323–338. https://doi.org/10.1080/15374416.2013.828297.

Collins, K. T. (2010). Advanced sampling designs in mixed research: Current practices and emerging trends in the social and behavioral sciences. In A. Tashakkori & C. Teddlie (Eds.), *Sage handbook of mixed methods in social and behavioral research* (2nd ed., pp. 353–377). Thousand Oaks, CA: SAGE Publications.

Creswell, J. W. (2013). *Qualitative inquiry & research design: Choosing among five approaches* (3rd ed.). Thousand Oaks, CA: SAGE Publications.

Davis, B., Phelps, R., & Wells, K. (2004). Complicity: An introduction and a welcome. *Complicity: An International Journal of Complexity and Education*, *1*(1), 1–7.

Davis, B., & Sumara, D. (2008). *Complexity and education: Inquires into learning, teaching, and research*. New York, NY: Routledge.

Dewey, J. (1998). *Experience and education: The 60th anniversary edition*. West Lafayette, Indiana: Kappa Delta Pi.

Dillon, S. (February 7, 2011). Failing schools often keep principals in place. *The New York Times*. Retrieved from https://www.nytimes.com/2011/02/08/education/08education.html.

Edhlund, B., & McDougall, A. (2016). *NVivo 11 essentials*. Lulu. com. Retrieved from https://books.google.com/books?hl=en&lr=&id=hQObCwAAQBAJ&oi=fnd&pg=PA21&dq=NVIVO11&ots=45R6sfnbPt&sig=WHSMNjFnuujsmplkE0U0ziKwxbQ.

Eriksen, M., & Cunliffe, A. (2010). Relational leadership. *Complicity: An International Journal of Complexity and Education, 7*(2), 97–100.

Follett, M. P. (1924). *The creative experience*. Рипол Классик. Retrieved from https://books.google.com/books?hl=en&lr=&id=Eg8IAwAAQBAJ&oi=fnd&pg=PR9&dq=Follett+1924+The+creative+experience&ots=QaeUj_06P4&sig=cPjCOvJcyFaD81hG9xfUkEDfQV0.

Gilstrap, D. (2005). Strange attractors and human interaction: Leading complex organizations through the use of metaphors. *Complicity: An International Journal of Complexity and Education, 2*(1), 55–69.

Graham, P. (Ed.). (1995). *Mary Parker Follett: Prophet of management: A celebration of writings from the 1920s*. Boston: Harvard Business School Press.

Grotzer, T. (2012). *Learning causality in a complex world: Understandings of consequence*. Lanham: Rowman & Littlefield Education.

Heissel, J. A., & Ladd, H. F. (2017). School turnaround in North Carolina: A regression discontinuity analysis. *Economics of Education Review*. https://doi.org/10.1016/j.econedurev.2017.08.001.

Higgins, J., & Bonne, L. (2011). Configurations of instructional leadership enactments that promote the teaching and learning of mathematics in a New Zealand elementary school. *Educational Administration Quarterly, 47*(5), 794–825.

Holland, J. H. (2014). *Complexity: A very short introduction*. New York, NY: Oxford University Press.

Jäppinen, A. I. K. A. (2014). Collaborative educational leadership: The emergence of human interactional sense-making process as a complex system. *Complicity: An International Journal of Complexity and Education, 11*(2), 65–85.

Johnson, J. (2013). The human factor. *Educational Leadership, 70*(7), 16–21.

Jordan, M. E. (2010). Mathematics as a complex system: Learning in complex adaptive systems. *Complicity: An International Journal of Complexity and Education, 7*(1), 70–76.

Jörg, T. (2011). *New thinking in complexity for the social sciences and humanities—A generative, transdisciplinary approach*. New York: Springer Publishers.

Jörg, T. (2014). The crisis of knowing in the age of complexity. In M. E. Jennec (Ed.), *Knowledge, discovery, transfer, and management in the age of transformation* (pp. 1–19). Hershey, PA: IGI Global.

Jörg, T. (2016). Opening the wonderous world of the possible for education: A generative complexity approach. In M. Koopmans & D. Stamovlasis (Eds.), *Complex dynamical system in education: Concepts, methods and applications* (pp. 59–92). Switzerland: Springer International Publishing.

Koopmans, M. (2016). Investigating the long memory process in daily high school attendance data. In M. Koopmans & D. Stamovlasis (Eds.), *Complex dynamical systems in education: Concepts, methods, and applications* (pp. 299–321). Switzerland: Springer International Publishing.

Koopmans, M., & Stamovlasis, D. (Eds.). (2016). *Complex dynamical systems in education: Concepts, methods and applications*. Switzerland: Springer International Publishing.

Kouzes, J. M., & Posner, B. Z. (1987). *The leadership challenge: How to get extraordinary things done in organizations*. San Francisco, CA: Jossey-Bass.

Kouzes, J. M., & Posner, B. Z. (2002). *The leadership challenge* (3rd ed.). San Francisco, CA: Jossey-Bass.

Leithwood, K., Seashore Louis, K., Anderson, S., & Wahlstrom, K. (2004). *Review of research: How leadership influences student learning* (Report). University of Minnesota, Center for Applied Research and Educational Improvement. Retrieved from http://conservancy.umn.edu/handle/11299/2035.

Lincoln, Y. S., & Guba, E. G. (1985). *Naturalistic inquiry*. Beverly Hills: Sage Publications.

Malloy, J., & Leithwood, K. (2017). Effects of distributed leadership on school academic press and student achievement. In K. Leithwood, J. Sun, & K. Pollock (Eds.), *How school leaders contribute to student success: The four paths framework* (pp. 69–91). Cham: Springer International Publishing. https://doi.org/10.1007/978-3-319-50980-8_5.

Marzano, R. J., Waters, T., & McNulty, B. A. (2005). *School leadership that works*. Alexandria, VA: ASCD.

Mason, M. (2008). What is complexity theory and what are its implications for educational change? *Educational Philosophy and Theory, 40*(1), 35–49.

McAlister, S. (2013). Why community engagement matters in school turnaround. *Voices in Urban Education, 36*, 35–42.

McClellan, J. L. (2010). Leadership and complexity: Implications for practice within the advisement leadership bodies at colleges and universities. *Complicity: An International Journal of Complexity and Education, 7*(2), 32–51.

McQuillan, P., & Kershner, B. (2018). Urban school leadership and adaptive change: The "Rabbit Hole" of continuous emergence. In A. J. Morales, C. Gershenson, D. Braha, A. A. Minai, & Y. Bar-Yam (Eds.), *Unifying themes in complex systems IX* (pp. 386–397). Springer International Publishing.

Mowat, E., & Davis, B. (2010). Interpreting embodied mathematics using network theory: Implication for mathematics education. *Complicity: An International Journal of Complexity and Education, 7*(1), 1–31.

Northouse, P. G. (2016). *Leadership: Theory and practice* (7th ed.). Thousand Oaks, CA: SAGE Publications.

Osberg, D., Biesta, G., & Cilliers, P. (2008). From representation to emergence: Complexity's challenge to the epistemology of schooling. *Educational Philosophy and Theory, 40*(1), 213–227.

Pennings, H. J. M., & Mainhard, T. (2016). Analyzing teacher-student interactions with state space grids. In M. Koopmans & D. Stamovlasis (Eds.), *Complex dynamical systems in education*. Switzerland: Springer International Publishing.

Player, D., & Katz, V. (2016). Assessing school turnaround: Evidence from Ohio. *The Elementary School Journal, 116*(4), 675–698.

Roueche, P. E. D., Baker III, G. A., & Rose, R. R. (2014). *Shared vision: Transformational leadership in American community colleges*. Rowman & Littlefield.

Schmidt-Davis, J., & Bottoms, G. (2012). *Turnaround high school principals: Recruit, prepare and empower leaders of change. High schools that work*. Southern Regional Education Board (SREB).

Shatzer, R. H., Caldarella, P., Hallam, P. R., & Brown, B. L. (2014). Comparing the effects of instructional and transformational leadership on student achievement: Implications for practice. *Educational Management Administration & Leadership, 42*(4), 445–459. https://doi.org/10.1177/1741143213502192.

Stamovlasis, D. (2016). Nonlinear dynamical interaction patterns in collaborative groups: Discourse analysis with orbital decomposition. In M. Koopmans & D. Stamovlasis (Eds.), *Complex dynamical systems in education* (pp. 273–297). Switzerland: Springer International Publishing.

Stanley, D. (2006). Comparative dynamics: Healthy collectivities and pattern which connects. *Complicity: An International Journal of Complexity and Education, 3*(1), 73–82.

Strese, S., Keller, M., Flatten, T. C., & Brettel, M. (2016). CEOs' passion for inventing and radical innovations in SMEs: The moderating effect of shared vision. *Journal of Small Business Management*, n/a-n/a. https://doi.org/10.1111/jsbm.12264.

Strunk, K. O., Marsh, J. A., Hashim, A. K., Bush-Mecenas, S., & Weinstein, T. (2016). The impact of turnaround reform on student outcomes: Evidence and insights from the Los Angeles Unified School District. *Education Finance and Policy*.

System [Def. 1]. (2015). *Dictionary.com*. Retrieved from http://dictionary.reference.com/browse/system?s=t.

Tan, C. Y. (2018). Examining school leadership effects on student achievement: The role of contextual challenges and constraints. *Cambridge Journal of Education, 48*(1), 21–45. https://doi.org/10.1080/0305764X.2016.1221885.

Uhl-Bien, M., & Marion, R. (Eds.). (2008). *Complexity leadership: Part I: Conceptual foundations*. Charlotte, NC: Information Age Publishing.

Vale, C., Davies, A., Weaven, M., Hooley, N., Davidson, K., & Loton, D. (2010). Leadership to improve mathematics outcomes in low SES schools and school networks. *Mathematics Teacher Education and Development, 12*(2), 47–71.

van Vondel, S., Steenbeck, H., van Dijk, M., & van Geert, P. (2016). "Looking at" educational interventions: Surplus value of a complex dynamic systems approach to study the effectiveness of a science and technology educational intervention. In M. Koopmans & D. Stamovlasis (Eds.), *Complex dynamical systems in education*. Switzerland: Springer International Publishing.

Vaughn, S., Schumm, J. S., & Sinagub, J. (1996). *Focus group interviews in education and psychology*. Thousand Oaks, CA: SAGE Publications, Inc.

Vygotsky, L. S. (1978). *Mind in society: The development of higher psychological processes* (M. Cole, V. John-Steiner, S. Scribner, & E. Souberman, Eds.). Cambridge, MA: Harvard University Press.

Chapter 4

School Leaders' Reflective Blogs Inspire Systemic Change
A Narrative Inquiry
Rita J. Hartman, Cheryl Burleigh, and James Lane

Reform efforts focused on high-stakes testing and top-down remedies have little or no effect in generating positive, systemic change and reinforcing the need for an alternative approach to school improvement (Bower & Parsons, 2016; Laici & Orlandini, 2016; Rose, 2015; Morante-Brock, 2014). In other words, educators experience limited success when large school changes are the outcome of federal, state, and district/school-level mandates, educational laws, and other outside forces.

The Every Student Succeeds Act of 2015 aimed at providing more autonomy to state and local public educational systems; nonetheless, U.S. public school districts still depend on state mandated assessment testing to gauge student success and motivate school change (James et al., 2016). Rather than reacting to government mandates or other outside influences, the five school leaders in this study initiated practical changes that surfaced from empathetic understanding of students' daily school experiences.

A positive and successful school culture is often situated in organizational integrity, where decisions and actions are based on ethical practices and the values represented by the whole school community and reflect a culturally responsive teaching and learning environment. These actions can lead to a positive climate and an increase in student academic success (Khalifa, Gooden, & Davis, 2016; Kılıçoğlu, 2017).

A school culture includes the interactions of both adults and students. Often the characteristics of a successful school culture focus on the adult relationships that include teachers, school leaders, and other school personnel. Adult characteristics that may help create a positive school culture adaptive to change are collaboration, a community of learning, supportive resources, and a focus on student academic success (Tichnor-Wagner, Harrison, & Vogel, 2016).

The school culture as defined from the student perspective often centers on student achievement and student responsibility where students take ownership in their own progress, collaborate with other students, openly dialogue with faculty, and take pride in their successes (Tichnor-Wagner et al., 2016). Instead of education becoming a *means to an end* driven by high-stakes testing, education becomes a platform for developing socially conscious individuals capable of informed decision-making within a community of learners (Erikson & Cooper, 2017). An additional component that should be added to this framework is the concept of student empowerment, in which student leadership and participation become integral components of the school culture (Horn, 2017; Kirk et al., 2015).

Empathetic design thinking is a process through which school leaders gather and analyze information to implement "hacks" or small changes within their school community (Carmel-Gilfilen & Portillo, 2016; Daniel, 2015; Eslamifar, 2014). The perceptions and insights on which school leaders reflected were based on their direct observations of what changes were needed to improve the learning environment for the unique needs of each school community. Empathetic design is a process that allowed the school leaders to embrace the changes needed based on not only their observations, but also the suggestions brought forth by teachers and students.

A key to a positive, supportive school culture is an empathetic understanding of the lived experiences of students who navigate the complexity of the school environment (Alant, Geyer, & Verde, 2015; Hartman, Johnston, & Hall, 2017). A systems-thinking approach motivated by empathetic observations is foundational in generating innovative school change analyzing the status quo, redesigning the existing functions, and building connections influencing all aspects of the school environment (Shaked & Schechter, 2017).

As school leaders found, changing an isolated event had ramifications throughout the school day. Schools are complex organizations with interrelationships producing a dynamic system where one small hack can create ripples of change in the school and in the school community (Koral Kordova, Frank, & Nissel Miller, 2018).

Educators must spend time gaining knowledge inside their schools and through their students' learning experiences to transcend centralized decision-making and implement systematic change (Laici & Orlandini, 2016). Using the insights and knowledge acquired by implementing "hacks" at their respective sites, school leaders may gain a better understanding of how to systematically improve the school culture increasing student satisfaction and student academic achievement.

PURPOSE STATEMENT AND RESEARCH QUESTION

The purpose of the narrative inquiry was to explore and describe the stories of school leaders who implemented hacks (small innovations) within their schools to gain a deeper understanding of the change process within a school environment. By spending time experiencing the day of a student, gathering and analyzing information, and reflecting on the experience in a public blog, school leaders were able to generate innovative change within their schools (Carmel-Gilfilen & Portillo, 2016; Daniel, 2015; Eslamifar, 2014; Kolko, 2010).

As researchers, we sought to explore the school leaders' observations of the students' daily experiences that motivated the initiations of a "hack" within each respective school site. This led us to this research question: *What changes did school leaders employ at their school site based on their empathic observations of student daily experiences?*

METHOD

To better understand the stories of school leaders implementing the hacks, a narrative inquiry approach was applied. Data was gathered through phone interviews with five school leaders who shadowed a student for the day during the 2016–2017 school year and posted their reflections of the experience on a public blog.

In agreement with Morgan-Fleming (2018), narrative inquiry provides a unique opportunity to examine the expertise of professionals in the daily application of their craft. This study focused on particular stories in which the researchers interacted with their participants to access a deeper understanding of their worlds. This study sought to understand not only the contents of these stories, but the *how* and *why* of the events they describe (Riessman & Speedy, 2018, p. 356).

As narrative researchers investigating an educational setting, the thinking on John Dewey was drawn upon. Dewey believed in the inextricable connection between personal experience and education (1938/1997). He viewed experience as the process through which both educators and educational institutions renewed themselves and called this "the re-creation of beliefs, ideals, hopes, happiness, misery, and practices."

"The continuity of any experience, through renewing of the social group, is a literal fact. Education, in its broadest sense, is the means of this social continuity of life" (Dewey, 1916/1944, p. 2). The researchers believe that the school leaders whose stories were captured demonstrated the essence of

Dewey's beliefs as they described the ways they applied their experiences to shape their schools' cultural and learning environments.

Clandinin and Connelly (2000) have cited Dewey as central to their understanding of narrative inquiry. Clandinin and colleagues (2016) described Dewey's (1938/1997) two criteria of experience, the "interaction and continuity enacted in situations," as the basis for "a narrative conception of experience" (p. 15). Clandinin and Connelly explained, "Simply put, narrative experience is the study of experience understood" (p. 15). As the experiences of these school leaders who were attempting to change the infrastructure and culture of their schools were gathered, the interaction and interconnectedness of the individuals around them became apparent (Clandinin et al., 2006).

The study sought to understand the challenges and complexities of these scenarios, each both unique and representative of the diverse landscape of American education. By exploring these experiences with and through the participants, aspects of their actions that might have been previously hidden to them and those around them would be discovered (Chase, 2018). These hidden elements will be revealed in the themes identified in this study.

Riessman (2008) noted that storytelling is dynamic and interactive, providing the teller a chance to make sense of the past. We figuratively walked with the tellers as they strived to make sense of their work. Schools and their various actors hold many stories. Per Riessman, "Narrative is everywhere" (p. 4). A few of those stories were captured to share.

PARTICIPANTS

The context for the study was the Shadow a Student Challenge and the geographic location was an online environment. The population was five school leaders who participated in the 2016–2017 Shadow a Student Challenge. The sample was drawn from individuals who self-selected to participate in response to email addresses posted at the Shadow a Student Challenge public website. Participants signed and returned an Informed Consent Form before the interviews.

The sample consisted of participants who were school leaders who had posted their reflections after shadowing a student on a public blog, had implemented a hack as a result of reflections gained from experiencing a student's day, and had experience with empathetic design thinking. Two men and three women shared their personal experiences implementing hacks. The school leaders were based in the United States and overseas and comprised of one superintendent, one high school principal, one middle school principal, and two elementary principals.

DATA COLLECTION

Phone interviews were conducted with a purposeful sample of five school leaders who took part in the Shadow a Student Challenge during the 2016–2017 school year and implemented an innovative hack based on the empathic reflections on their shadowing experience. Transcriptions of the interviews were sent to the participants for a members' check to make sure their comments were accurately represented. Saturation, where no new ideas were evident, was reached after five interviews. Content analysis approach was utilized because it is more flexible than other types of analysis and allows researchers to describe the data in a more systematic way (Finfgeld-Connett, 2013; White & Marsh, 2006).

DATA ANALYSIS

A process of inductive, thematic coding was applied in close analyses of stories to gain insight into the experiences of the study participants (Riessman, 2008). Team members read separately, then compared notes as we read text generated from interviews, followed by thorough analysis of the data. Jacobs (2014) has noted that hermeneutics can expose meanings of organizational culture. An inductive process was applied and included a hermeneutic circle to gain a holistic understanding, compared first impressions with other team members, units of meaning were found, and synthesized our findings (Ziegler, Paulus, & Woodside, 2006).

In this way, a hermeneutic focus was applied to draw broader meanings from our texts (Chase, 2018). Four colors in the Word document were used to highlight codes and themes (Johnston, Rasmusson, Foyil, & Shopland, 2017). Throughout analytic memos (Saldana & Omasta, 2018) were kept to capture the researchers' thinking during analysis and their recursive reading of the texts. Interpretations of each text were discussed several times and those memos were utilized to record and refine thinking.

Transcripts were divided into responses of between one and three sentences. Each section or stanza was then numbered. Following that, each researcher read the transcript and identified sequences of words that represented what Riessman (2006) calls "idea units" (p. 33). These were the units of analytical focus. From there, the units were condensed into more general codas or themes. As the transcripts were read and reread recursively, similarities in overarching themes were identified. Some themes were more dominant in individual transcripts.

Similarities with other transcripts were identified, when possible, and were combined into more general themes. Chase (2018) stressed that in narrative analysis, prior theory or conceptual framework must serve as a lens through which to interpret narratives. Emerging themes were identified by checking against a conceptual frame of empathetic design and sought to understand how these practitioners demonstrated the concepts of empathetic design in their work. Unique conceptual insights were also looked for. The researchers endeavored to be aware of larger constructs, what Riessman calls "power relations, hidden inequalities, and historical contingencies" (p. 76), making connections between the individual and the larger school culture.

Researchers have described the concept of seeking coherence in narrative inquiry, both within and between stories (Riessman, 2008; Chase, 2018). Chase (2018) joined other researchers (Salmon & Riessman, 2013; Frank, 2012; Hyvarinen, Hyden, Saarheimo, & Tamboukou, 2010) in questioning whether it is the stories that seek coherence or rather the researchers driven by their own biases. The researchers asked themselves whether they as listeners were seeking coherence, rather than allowing it to emerge from the data.

They understand and acknowledge this issue. They also recognize that as experienced school administrators, each of them bring background knowledge and bias to these stories. They have sought to identify coherence where they believe it exists in the data and to describe insights as parts of a meaningful whole.

RESULTS: PARTICIPANT NARRATIVE SUMMARIES

This study focused on specific changes that school leaders made in the infrastructure of their schools after shadowing one or more of their students. Following is a brief description of each leader, identified by a pseudonym and summary of the change he or she enacted.

May

May was a school superintendent who shadowed two students. She shadowed a high school student who was commuting eighty miles daily on a school bus between the base school and a vocational school. She noted that the schedule disrupted the students' meals at school. They were not able to eat breakfast at school, and their lunch was delayed. As a result, she changed the cafeteria staff schedule, so the students could eat both breakfast and lunch. She also shadowed a third-grade student with reading problems.

Finding the reading interventions inadequate, May helped research and implement a corrective reading program for grades three through middle school. Because she found her own experience so rewarding, May required the district administrative team of ten administrators to shadow a student.

Following that, she implemented a pattern of ten different teachers shadowing students each year. A result was that all teachers shadowed each other, and some students were asking to be shadowed.

Stanley

Stanley was a middle school principal whose shadowing experience convinced him that his school needed to become more developmentally responsive to the needs of the students. He observed that the existing advisory program had grown stagnant and ineffective, becoming more of a homeroom than a productive period to improve student academic and social experiences on campus. The advisory classes could have as many as twenty-five students, making it difficult to develop meaningful connections with students. The advisory program was also at the beginning of the school day, so it became an expendable time for students who arrived late to school.

Often teachers who were running late to school asked their colleagues to cover their advisory class for them; thus, little meaningful class instruction was taking place during the advisory period. In response, Stanley revised the structure of the advisory program so that each of the school's teachers was assigned students from different grades during the advisory class period to balance the number of students per teacher throughout the school lowering the student number. The result was lowering the number of students in each advisory class.

By having a smaller class size during advisory, teachers were able to effectively deliver the advisory program content and spend quality time with each of the students. The advisory period was also moved to follow third period. Students were always expected to be at school by 7:45 a.m., the start of the school day, but now a content area class started the school day instead of the advisory period.

Monthly themes were developed for the advisory program which coincided with monthly district-wide and national initiatives, for example red ribbon week. The new structure enabled students to interact with teachers with whom they may not have had a connection. The result was a renewed focus on forging personal connections with students and implementing developmentally appropriate activities to enrich the school experience for students.

Beth

Beth was an elementary principal who shadowed a student with special needs. She observed how disrupted the day was for special needs students who were continually being pulled out of their classrooms to receive individual support. She also realized how much these students wanted to be treated equally with their peers. As a result, Beth initiated an inclusive co-teaching model, with the classroom teacher and the special education teacher planning and working together so all the services could be provided within the classroom.

Transitioning to the co-teaching model created a positive change and transformed the school from a divided staff to a culture in which special education teachers and classroom teachers communicated and collaborated with each other. Special education teachers began to teach lessons to the whole class and began to invite the principal, assistant principal, and others to observe.

Trevor

Trevor was a high school principal who implemented three major changes as a result of his shadowing experience. He became aware of the amount of stress his students were experiencing in the push toward academic achievement, state testing, and a rigorous school schedule, in addition to other obligations outside of school. As a result, Trevor implemented a forty-five-minute period of time once a month with nine different session options in which students could select "fun" or relaxing activities to help lower some of their stress.

Another issue Trevor became aware of was the time students spent inactively sitting during the school day. He thus began encouraging teachers to move away from teacher-directed activities to more active student-led learning in which students were in groups problem-solving and collaborating. Finally, he added eighteen new courses the following school year, all focused on project-based, real-life learning, including job shadowing and internships designed to connect student interests with real-life opportunities after high school.

Laura

Laura was an elementary school principal for an international school in Southeast Asia. Her shadowing experience made her aware that the school needed to improve its classroom open-door policy. The message given to parents at orientation and at meetings was that there was an open-door policy, but the reality was that parents and community members needed to make an appointment with the teacher to visit the school or classroom. Heavy classroom double doors were kept closed. In addition, she reflected on the process where teachers were being observed by a traditional protocol of administrators entering the classroom by a scheduled appointment and then conducting an observation of teaching practices.

Teacher growth opportunities to improve teaching practices, delivery of instructional content, and interaction with students were limited to only feedback provided by administrators. Laura realized student and teacher interactions with one another and the school community needed to change to encourage communication and bring about a more open school learning environment. As a result, she enacted a peer walkthrough program for teachers to give feedback to each other. She encouraged individuals within the school community to visit the school campus.

Teachers began to leave their doors open and post Twitter hashtags such as "observe me" as an open invitation to enter their classrooms. Laura arranged for teachers to have ninety-minute collaborative planning sections within the school day for teachers to share their observations of others' classrooms. Therefore, Laura was able to move her school from a traditional structure of administrative feedback to a peer-focused collaborative learning environment.

SCHOOL CULTURE WITH DOMINANT THEMES: NURTURING AWARENESS, BUILDING RELATIONSHIPS, AND ENACTING CHANGE OVERARCHING

An overarching motif of culture permeated the results of this study. Each participant affected the culture of his or her work environment intellectually, emotionally, and physically. The concept was reiterated in the stories of each participant through the key themes of nurturing awareness, building relationships, and enacting change. Each theme was supported by several situation-specific subthemes distributed unevenly across stories.

For example, Trevor's implementation of high school courses based on student collaboration showed subthemes of student empowerment. His job shadowing and internship program for seniors reflected a subtheme of real-world application that did not appear in the other hacks. While specific to his project, it reflected the larger theme of enacting change.

In another example, Stanley's rebuilding of his middle school's student advisory program reflected a unique subtheme of developmental responsiveness that supported broader themes of nurturing awareness. Thus, although distributed unevenly across stories, subthemes supported the broader themes of nurturing awareness, building relationships, and enacting change. We discuss each theme in greater detail below.

Nurturing Awareness

The theme of nurturing awareness seemed to build synergistically on the triumvirate concepts of reflection, awareness, and empathy. Each participant was reflective and thoughtful, turning inward to consider what he or she could do to enact change. This would seem an obvious assumption, since their initial involvement in the project that spawned this study was to blog about their self-initiated experience of shadowing a student. Nonetheless, to enact change, each participant became aware of the situations of others, whether students or other staff. Finally, each demonstrated empathy, which was defined as the ability both intellectually and emotionally to understand the experiences of others.

The central effect of the shadowing experience is perhaps best reflected in this theme. The concept of nurturing awareness and its subthemes was clear. For example, in May's experience when shadowing a vocational student who commuted eighty miles each day between the base school and the school that provided a welding program, she observed that the students boarded the bus at the base school at 6:30 a.m. before the school breakfast was ready and returned to the base school between student lunch periods, which required them to wait longer to eat lunch.

While as superintendent May was aware of this structure, it was only when she experienced the event alongside the students that she became more deeply reflective, aware, and empathetic. As a result, she altered the work schedules of the cafeteria staff to prepare a "grab and go" breakfast for the students to eat on the bus and to serve the students lunch when they returned.

In another experience, May's shadowing of a third grader revealed to her the inadequacies of the school's remedial reading program. Her observation captured the essence of the nurturing awareness theme: "How could this be happening? How could we be sitting here allowing this? What are we going to do about it?"

Trevor similarly demonstrated awareness of the effects of the pressure of academic achievement on students in his hack to create school time for students to participate in a "fun," nonacademic activity. He based his plan to implement more active learning strategies on this insight: "When the butt gets numb, the brain gets dumb." Stanley, a middle school principal, reflected the views of all participants when he said, "This is what education needs, this is what the world needs, to spend time with others and understanding each other's worlds."

Building Relationships

Naturally flowing from the theme of awareness emerged the theme of building relationships. The broad theme was supported by the subthemes of communication, feedback, collaboration, and empowerment. When considering these stories, it seemed that one subtheme merged symbiotically into the next. These leaders began their change projects by communicating—with students, teachers, staff, parents, and the broader school community.

They did so first through blogs connected to an earlier project. Their modes of communication continued to evolve, however, resulting in the manifestations of their hacks. Embedded within communication was feedback, which implied dialogue, progressing to collaboration and then empowerment. As with the projects themselves, empowerment took different forms.

Stanley communicated his transformation of the student advisory program through social media and the school newsletter. By entering into dialogue with a special needs student, Beth realized the desire these students shared to become as empowered as their mainstreamed peers. As a result of this dialogue, Beth implemented a co-teaching model that encouraged collaboration among special education and content teachers. This additionally empowered the special education teachers as they worked with content teachers to shape curriculum.

As a result, she said, "Teachers are communicating with each other, where in the past they did not engage with the rest of the staff." Trevor empowered students to take control of their learning through project-based learning, job shadowing, and internships. Laura publicized her expanded walkthrough strategy through her blog, the school magazine, and school newspaper. As a result of her shadowing experience, Laura expanded the school policy of walkthroughs to engage the entire faculty.

A strategy that had been traditionally an administrative practice became a commonplace for the entire school. Laura spoke of "the fertilization of ideas." Trevor's reflection encapsulates the key concepts of the building relationships theme: "People talk about that they want to be a part of something that is innovative and makes sense for our students."

Enacting Change

Not surprisingly, the third dominant theme that emerged from this study was enacting change. This may seem self-evident, since the intent of the study was for administrators to reflect on a school change they had implemented. As with the two previous themes of nurturing awareness and building relationships, however, probing their stories of enacting change revealed deeper subthemes. Change was demonstrated in two modes. First was a physical change in the infrastructure. May changed the schedule of the cafeteria staff. Trevor implemented new courses. Beth expanded the school walkthrough program. Laura instituted deeper collaboration among teachers. Stanley revamped his school advisory program.

While significant, these changes in infrastructure evolved into even more dramatic changes in the mind-sets of each school faculty, who became more receptive to, and in some cases expectant of, cultural change. Stanley's faculty renewed their commitments to forge personal connections with their students. Trevor's staff became committed to seeking positive changes.

He observed, "People love our culture, but at the same time if there are opportunities that are more engaging and make more sense for students, they are going to start to look at those." After expanding the walkthrough program, Laura found teachers eager to embrace the change. She observed, "The art of the walkthrough has changed quite a bit. I am now asked to cover classes to allow teachers the freedom to get out and see other classes which is, I guess, a huge, shift in the culture of the school."

As a superintendent, May developed a teacher shadowing program that transformed the district culture. She observed, "At the division level each year, we have 10 different teachers shadow, and the following year 10 different teachers, the next year an additional 10, and so on. So, I think this has changed the culture."

As noted earlier, because each hack was unique, some subthemes appeared in the stories of individual participants, but not in all. The subtheme of real-world applications was clear in Trevor's hacks, as he established workplace, job shadowing, and internship programs for seniors. His actions also demonstrated student empowerment and active learning, through his creation of eighteen new courses based on project-based learning.

Stanley demonstrated developmental responsiveness through revamping his student advisory program to better meet the emotional needs of his middle schoolers. Each of these unique demonstrations combined to create a larger pattern of change by our participants. Each was willing to effect a change in his or her school's infrastructure, which in turn created a broader culture of change in the school staff's efforts to meet the needs of their students.

FINDINGS

By immersing themselves in the role of a student for the day, school leaders developed an empathetic understanding of some of the challenges students navigate during their daily school routine. Using the insights and knowledge acquired by implementing hacks at their respective school sites, school leaders gained a better understanding of how to improve the school environment and culture resulting in an increase in student satisfaction and potentially student academic success.

From the content analysis, the overarching theme of culture emerged supported by the five main themes. In each of the schools, the school leaders influenced the school culture by implementing a hack that generated a positive, supportive, community reflected in the adult relationships, the student-adult relationships, and student empowerment. Under culture, the five themes of nurturing awareness, building relationships, and enacting change arose.

Nurturing awareness was reflected in the way each school leader approached the Shadow a Student Challenge project experience, being open to seeing the school day through the eyes of a student and having an empathetic understanding of some of the challenges students encountered.

School leaders understood the importance of building relationships by communicating, providing feedback, collaborating, and cultivating a sense of empowerment among all the stakeholders in the school environment. The third theme was enacting change which occurred through physical changes in the infrastructure and through changes in the mind-sets of the school faculty at each site who become open and embracing of the change. The following additional subthemes were unique to the specific school setting: real-world application, active learning, and developmentally responsive.

Systems thinking used to implement changes within schools based on school leaders' observations inspired systemic change which may contribute to a broader district and countywide improvements to student learning. The "hacks" implemented at each respective school site was solely based on the observations of the school leaders who participated in this study. Other school staff and educators were not involved in the Shadow a Student program nor observed the students to formulate the changes employed to improve school culture.

CONCLUSION

Each of the hacks the participants enacted improved the culture of their schools. In addition, the changes impacted their schools' public relations efforts and seemed to have created significant positive effects on their school-community relationships. One assumption is that when changes at school create positive changes in students' attitudes, the relationships among the school and its various constituents, especially parents, improve. In addition, however, several participants applied public relations strategies to communicate these positive changes directly to parents and other external school stakeholders. Specific examples are discussed below.

When Stanley moved the advisory program to third period, students felt more pressured to arrive on time. This, he said, "forced a conversation with parents. I took them out of their comfort zone, and I was OK with that." To promote the program, he initiated a Sunday newsletter for parents describing the program and the monthly theme and activities. "These are some of the things we push out to parents. What is advisory? We are having a video on this, we are discussing that. Your kids are getting organized and learning to manage their time." This practice, he concluded, "helps communicate with parents who say, 'I don't know what is going on in that school.'"

Through one of May's hacks, administrators and teachers began shadowing students. In a direct communication to teachers and the community, she asked her administrators to blog about their shadowing experiences. She noted, "I know teachers like the process." This practice demonstrates another positive effect of the hack on school public relations.

Laura changed the process of teacher observations and walkthroughs to encourage teachers to engage in more peer observations. To prepare teachers and parents for the project, she engaged in several activities to promote the program. She posted a blog on the school site, wrote an article for the school magazine, and granted an interview to the local newspaper. By the time the program was fully implemented, she said, "Some teachers got into the habit of posting on the door a Twitter hashtag #observeme, giving feedback through a different medium, social media."

Beth moved her school's special education program from a pullout model to an inclusive, co-teaching model. "Teachers are communicating with each other, where in the past they did not engage with the rest of the staff. That alone has made a huge difference in the culture of the school for staff, parents, and students." Unfortunately, however, positive impact is not always easy to quantify and communicate to policy makers outside the school.

She acknowledged that the program is more expensive, since it requires more teachers and admits, "It is hard to show at the community level, those not in the school, the impact of what we are trying to do." A public relations imperative is to make "a bigger push to see the benefits of the process and to show people this." She acknowledges a challenge faced by all school administrators: "My only concern is how to quantify the data. There is more to that, including looking at the whole child and how we are impacting them. We are still struggling in how to show this."

In a move that made a direct impact on his community, Trevor implemented a career outreach program of job shadowing and internships in order for students to get out in the workplace. One goal of the program was to "fine-tune some of those soft skills that employers really need. Employers have a hard time articulating their needs when it comes to the specific skills, but the soft skills are something that we can work on."

He notes that one result of this and other new programs was that "the parents and school board are supportive and a great team. It's not perfect, and we still have room to grow, but our community trusts our school district. We operate very transparently and collaboratively with them. We are very fortunate." That would seem to be the penultimate goal of any school program and its effect on public relations. Clearly an overarching recommendation would be to reach out to the school community and publicize successful changes through all media, as well as by building relationships by encouraging outside participation in the work of the school.

Each narrative offered a glimpse into the daily aspects of school culture where educators consider what is needed to provide a learning environment that is safe, where learning is meaningful, and where students feel their contributions will enhance their academic and social experiences. In other words, this describes a school cultural setting in which students want to attend, learn, and be productive members of the community.

Educators and school leaders can benefit by viewing the school experience from the student's perspective and using the insights and knowledge gained to create hacks or small innovations, leading to a positive shift in the school culture and the values and beliefs permeated throughout the school. Expanded research may include analysis of cultural diversity, socioeconomics, community involvement, variety of academic courses offered, and intervention programs available within the school to assist in identifying students who may be at risk of academic failure.

The findings of this study may provide school leaders with a deeper understanding of the importance of being empathetic to student needs and the importance of including systems thinking and change to improve the students' learning environment. The study found that school culture plays a prominent role in predicting educators' and school leaders' capacity for successfully changing the school learning environment. The study revealed the importance of developing and implementing a supportive school culture to improve a school's capacity for change. The results further reinforce the need for continuous school improvement and thorough integration of a positive and deepening support system for the school community.

The process is sustained through continuous collaboration between educators and school leaders not only to employ change within the school culture, but also to maintain and nurture the school's capacity for change. This could only have been revealed through the narrative stories of the innovative school leaders who participated in this study. The results of the study may also add to the body of knowledge on school reform, empathetic design, systems thinking, and innovative change.

These school leaders used the insights they gained and the empathy they felt from the shadowing experience to generate innovative actions meeting specific needs at each of their schools. The changes often resulted in the allocation or reallocation of resources. It is not clear from the school leaders' stories how the logistics of the innovations unfolded. Three of the school leaders introduced new programs requiring additional personnel, program purchases or program development, and staff development. May initiated a corrective reading program.

Stanley reenergized an advisory program. Beth activated a co-teaching model. Trevor targeted building eighteen new courses for the following school year, and Laura introduced a peer observation process where every teacher is able to visit every classroom.

There were also schedule changes that occurred rapidly with the innovations. May changed the lunchtime for the cafeteria staff to accommodate a scheduling issue with students returning to campus from another site. Stanley moved advisory base from the beginning of school to after third period, and Trevor changed the school schedule to add a relaxation period once a month. These changes involved significant manipulations of school infrastructure—the mechanics of which were beyond the parameters of this study.

The innovation at each of the school sites was initiated by an inspired school leader who lived the day as a student, gained empathy for students' experiences, and was able to find the resources to generate positive change at his or her school. It would be interesting to revisit the five schools over the next few years to observe how the various innovations have been maintained and supported with resources of energy, time, and money.

REFERENCES

Alant, E., Geyer, S., & Verde, M. (2015). Developing empathetic skills among teachers and learners in high schools in Tshwane: An inter-generational approach involving people with dementia. *Perspectives in Education, 33*(3), 141–158.

Betts, F. (November, 1992). How systems thinking applies to education. *Improving School Quality, 50*(3), 38–41.

Bower, H. A., Parsons, E. R., & Carlton, E. R. (2016). Teacher identity and reform: Intersections within school culture. *The Urban Review, 48*(5), 743–765.

Carmel-Gilfilen, C., & Portillo, M. (2016). Designing with empathy. *HERD: Health Environments Research & Design Journal, 9*(2), 130–146. doi: 1177/1937586715592633.

Chase, S. E. (2018). Narrative inquiry. In N. K. Denzin & Y. S. Lincoln (Eds.), *The SAGE handbook of qualitative research* (5th ed, pp. 546–560). Thousand Oaks, CA: SAGE.

Clandinin, D. J., Caine, V., Lessard, S., & Huber, J. (2016). *Engaging in narrative inquiries with children and youth.* San Francisco, CA: Jossey-Bass.

Clandinin, D. J., & Connelly, F. M. (2000). *Narrative inquiry: Experience and story in qualitative research.* San Francisco, CA: Jossey-Bass.

Clandinin, D. J., Huber, J., Huber, M., Murphy, S. M., Orr, A. M., Pearce, M., & Steeves, P. (2006). *Composing diverse identities: Narrative inquiries into the interwoven lives of children and teachers.* New York, NY: Routledge.

Connelly, F. M., & Clandinin, D. J. (2006). Narrative inquiry. In J. Green, G. Camili, & P. Elmore (Eds.), *Handbook of complementary methods in education research* (pp. 477–487). Mahwah, NJ: Lawrence Erlbaum.

Daniel, S. M. (2015). Empathetic, critical integrations of multiple perspectives: A core practice for language teacher education? *TESOL Journal, 6*(1), 149–176.

Dewey, J. (1944). *Democracy and education: An introduction to the philosophy of education*. New York, NY: The Free Press (Original work published 1916).

Dewey, J. (1997). *Experience and education*. New York, NY: Touchstone (Original work published 1938).

Eriksen, M., & Cooper, K. (2017). Shared-purpose process: Implications and possibilities for student learning, development, and self-transformation. *Journal of Management Education, 41*(3), 385–414. doi: 10.1177/1052562917689890.

Eslamifar, A. (2014). *A tool for empathetic user experience design* (Doctoral dissertation). Retrieved from ProQuest Dissertations & Theses Global. (1570448).

Finfgeld-Connett, D. (2013). Use of content analysis to conduct knowledge-building and theory-generating qualitative systematic reviews. *Qualitative Research, 14*(3), 341–352. doi: 10.1177/1468794113481790.

Goldman, D., & Senge, P. (2014). *The triple focus: A new approach to education*. Florence, MA: More Than Sound.

Hartman, R. J., Johnston, E., & Hill, M. (2017). Empathetic design: A sustainable approach to school change. *Discourse and Communication for Sustainable Education, 8*(2), 38–56.

Horn, B. R. (2017). Eight voices of empowerment: Student perspectives in a restructured urban middle school. *Urban Education, 52*(4), 525–552. doi: 10.1177/0042085915574522.

Jacobs, A. H. M. (2014). Critical hermeneutics and higher education: A perspective on texts, meaning, and institutional culture. *South African Journal of Philosophy, 33*(3), 297–310. doi: 10.1080/02580136.2014.948327.

James, M. C., Rupley, W. H., Hall, K. K., Nichols, J. A., Rasinski, T. V., & Harmon, W. C. (2016). Reform stall: An ecological analysis of the efficacy of an urban school reform initiative to improve students' reading and mathematics achievement. *Cogent Education, 3*(1), 1245089. doi: 10.1080/2331186X.2016.1245089.

Johnston, E., Rasmusson, X., Foyil, B., & Shopland, P. (2017). Witnesses to transformation: Family member experiences providing individualized music to their relatives with dementia. *Cogent Education, 4*(1), 1362888. doi: 10.1080/2331186X.2017.1362888.

Khalifa, M. A., Gooden, M. A., & Davis, J. E. (2016). Culturally responsive school leadership: A synthesis of the literature. *Review of Educational Research, 86*(4), 1272–1311. doi: 10.3102/0034654316630383.

Kılıçoğlu, G. (2017). Consistency or discrepancy? Rethinking schools from organizational hypocrisy to integrity. *Management in Education, 31*(3), 118–124. doi: 10.1177/0892020617715268.

Kirk, C. M., Lewis, R. K., Brown, K., Karibo, B., Scott, A., & Park, E. (2015). The empowering schools project: Identifying the classroom and school characteristics that lead to student empowerment. *Youth & Society, 49*(6), 827–847. doi: 10.1177/0044118X14566118.

Kolko, J. (2010). Abductive thinking and sensemaking: The drivers of design synthesis. *Design Issues, 26*(1), 15–28. doi: 10.1162/desi.2010.26.1.15.

Koral Kordova, S., Frank, M., & Nissel Miller, A. (2018). Systems thinking education—Seeing the forest through the trees. *Systems, 6*(3), 29. doi: 10.3390/systems6030029.

Laici, C., & Orlandini, L. (2016). Avanguardie educative: Paths of innovation for schools. *Research on Education and Media, 8*(1), 53–61. doi: 10.1515/rem-2016-0007.

Lannon-Kim, C. (1991). Revitalizing the schools: A systems thinking approach. *The Systems Thinker, 2*(5), 1–5.

Merriam, S. B. (2009). *Qualitative research: A guide to design and implementation.* San Francisco, CA: Jossey-Bass.

Morante-Brock, S. (2014). *The common core state standards: School reform at three suburban middle schools* (Doctoral dissertation). Available from ProQuest Dissertations and Theses database. (3610426).

Moses, A. (n.d.). *What you should know about systems thinking.* Retrieved from https://asiasociety.org/what-you-should-know-about-systems-thinking.

Riessman, C. K. (2008). *Narrative methods for the human sciences.* Thousand Oaks, CA: SAGE.

Riessman, C. K., & Speedy, J. (2018). Narrative inquiry in the psychotherapy professions. In N. K. Denzin & Y. S. Lincoln (Eds.), *The SAGE handbook of qualitative research* (5th ed.), (pp. 427–456). Thousand Oaks, CA: SAGE.

Rose, M. (December 10, 2015). *School reform fails the test.* Retrieved from https://theamericanscholar.org/school-reform- fails-the-test/#.WfkRhGhSzIU.

Saldana, J., & Omasta, M. (2018). *Qualitative research: Analyzing life.* Thousand Oaks, CA: SAGE.

Shaked, H., & Schechter, C. (2017). Systems thinking among school middle leaders. *Educational Management Administration & Leadership, 45*(4), 699–718. doi: 10.1177/1741143215617949.

Tichnor-Wagner, A., Harrison, C., & Cohen-Vogel, L. (2016). Cultures of learning in effective high schools. *Educational Administration Quarterly, 52*(4), 602–642. doi: 10.1177/0013161X16644957.

U.S. Department of Education. Every Student Succeeds Act (ESSA), 2015. Retrieved from https://www.ed.gov/essa.

White, M. D., & Marsh, E. E. (2006). Content analysis: A flexible methodology. *Library Trends, 55*(1), 22–45. doi: 10.1353/lib.2006.0053.

Yin, R. K. (2013). *Case study research: Design and methods* (5th ed.). Thousand Oaks, CA: SAGE.

Ziegler, M., Paulus, T., & Woodside, M. (2006). Creating a climate of engagement in a blended learning environment. *Journal of Interactive Learning Research, 17*(3), 295–318.

Chapter 5

Resettled Muslim Parents' Perceptions of School-Community Relations

Michael E. Hess, Charles L. Lowery,
Rowda Olad, Connor Fewell,
Steven Yeager, and Tracy Kondrit

This study examines the perceptions of a resettled community of Somali Muslim parents in a major Midwest urban school district about school-community relations. As such, the investigation looked into how Somali parents with school-age children perceived school efforts to communicate with and involve them as parents, the responsiveness of the school to their children, and administrative efforts to improve the overall cultural connection with the Somali Muslim population.

Twelve Somali parents were interviewed using a semi-structured interview protocol that explored how they make meaning relating to issues impacting them as parents of school-age children. As a qualitative study, the study purposed to bring to the forefront the voices of a resettled community that is often overlooked or relegated to the margins of media and political discourse.

Additionally, results from the study could be used to further develop methods to improve school-to-home communication and school-community relations with immigrant and refugee families. These findings may be used to better inform school-community relationships in districts that serve refugee resettlements. By informing school administrators of the perceptions of resettled Somali Muslim families, schools can better provide meaningful communication and connections for these families and potentially gain transference into other resettled and immigrant populations.

CONTEXT OF STUDY

Background

Historically, Somalis have been immigrating to the United States and settling in urban areas as early as the 1920s (Putnam & Noor, 1993). A point important to this study is that, in the 1990s, the number of refugees escaping civil war in Somalia increased and they later settled in New York, Washington, DC, Los Angeles, San Diego, Atlanta, and Detroit (Putnam & Noor, 1993). During this time Somalia faced internal political turmoil that led to ongoing civil conflicts (Kallick & Mathema, 2016; Putnam & Noor, 1993; Swarns, 2003).

Due to that turmoil, the United States has seen an arrival of politically resettled individuals that have found asylum in many major metro areas, such as Minneapolis, Minnesota; Columbus, Ohio; Seattle, Washington; Washington, DC; San Diego, California; and Boston, Massachusetts (Kallick & Mathema, 2016). In addition, smaller Somali settlements have been established in Atlanta, Georgia; Phoenix, Arizona; Salt Lake City, Utah; Nashville, Tennessee; Memphis, Tennessee; and Lewiston, Maine (Kallick & Mathema, 2016; Nadeau, 2008; Nezer, 2013).

Undoubtedly, these areas have now experienced a significant enrollment of second and third generation Somali American students in their school systems. Predominantly these children are from Muslim families with strong ethnic and cultural ties and even stronger conservative religious convictions. Schools and the Somali students they serve find themselves in a web of relations and culture that has not only religious implications but also political, social, cultural, and more especially educational concerns.

Research Questions

Two primary research questions served as the basis for this qualitative study of Somali parents' perception of school-community relations with teachers and school leadership. The first asked, "What are the perceptions of Somali Muslim refugee parents regarding their expectations of the education of their children?" Secondarily, we inquired, "How do resettled Somali Muslim parents experience the education of their children in an urban area?" Specific to the ideas that underscore these overarching questions were concerns of how Somali parents perceive school-community relations, which include involvement of parents in the school setting, interactions of school administration with parents, and experiences with school culture.

Significance of the Study

A supportive school environment has been identified as a critical element in ensuring the well-being and belonging of children of refugee communities

(Bond et al., 2007; Correa-Velez, Gifford, & Barnett, 2010). By extension, the relationship between parent and schools has been linked to establishing a supportive school environment (Gaitan, 2012; Jeynes, 2003; Noguera, 2004; Zinth, 2005). While it is a general concern that schools establish such supportive climates, this becomes especially important for the needs of diverse and different populations. For example, the children of Muslim refugee families may face additional and unique issues in the school setting (Ahmad & Szpara, 2003; Guo, 2011; McBrien, 2015; Parker-Jenkins, 1991).

In this study, resettled Somali parents' perceptions of the relationships of refugee families with school leadership and staff, the importance of communication between school leadership and refugee families, and the related concepts of assimilation, acculturation, and language justice were explored. As Nezer (2013) has observed, anti-immigrant and anti-refugee legislation or state and local perspectives create unique challenges for refugee resettlement communities within the local school communities.

With this in mind, while resettled Somali families are well established in many of the nation's urban areas, these individuals face potential discrimination. Specifically, discrimination in the social and political milieu that relates to their identities, notably the social labeling they face as refugee, as Muslim, and as "black" (Darboe, 2003; Kallick & Mathema, 2016; Wingfield & Karaman, 2002).

LITERATURE REVIEW

According to McBrien (2015), "Children of refugee and voluntary immigrant families share the challenges of adapting to a new culture and, usually, learning a new language" (pp. 444–45). The parents of these children face the same types of challenges when it comes to being involved in their children's education. In McBrien's words, "The uniquely challenging combinations of circumstances faced by the small population of U.S. refugees have resulted in inadequate services [overall] to address the needs of these families" (p. 445).

For the purposes of this study the focus will be on how resettled Somali Muslim parents, as individuals with unique needs and challenges, view the school's relationship with them. In particular, the literature relevant to our findings concern school communication with Somali parents (Carlock, 2014), barriers for Somali parental involvement (Osman & Månsson, 2015), and issues of acculturation (Isik-Ercan, 2015) and assimilation (Darboe, 2003).

Somali Parents and Teacher/School Communication

As Robinson and Mazid (2016) have posited, "School organizations are grappling with social change and are not fully prepared to address the needs of students and families of difference" (p. 205). This observation becomes especially highlighted in relation to resettled families of diverse religious and linguistic backgrounds. In particular, four key tensions exist for Muslim families and with children in public schooling.

These tensions in school-community relations were classified as (1) identity and belonging, (2) discrimination, (3) values and attitudes, and (4) Islamic education (McCreery, Jones, & Holmes, 2007). McCreery and colleagues (2007) argued that by sending their children to schools that are faith-oriented, Muslim families find relief from the fears and apprehensions they experience in public school settings. However, resettled refugee and immigrant families do not always have the economic resources to make leaving public schools a choice (Huddleston & Wolffhardt, 2016; Segal & Mayadas, 2005).

Relating to communication are concerns of language justice and linguistic equity. Robinson and Mazid (2016) noted that "educational environments are no longer homogeneous, and educators must be adept at engaging and communicating with students and families from a wide range of circumstances" (p. 204). The way in which schools communicate and connect with parents through language is directly associated with how welcome parents feel. Equally important are the ways in which cultural events acknowledge the parent culture.

As Carlock (2014) has stated, "Parent engagement and disengagement often result from the social environments parents encounter at school" (p. 198). School administrators and other educators may perceive that resettled or immigrant parents in poverty do not participate in school functions due to a lack of concern about their children's education or due to their own lack of education (Carlock, 2014; Osman & Månsson, 2015).

Importantly, Carlock argued, "Less often do [school personnel] consider how school communications and events can make parents feel unwelcome" (p. 198). The connection between the use of language and parental agency in school engagement is inherently connected. Lack of materials and communication provided to parents in their native language can have an impact on how welcome and engaged parents feel. As Carlock (2014) noted, "If a person's language is not connected to the decision-making apparatus of a community, that person is effectively disempowered. This lack of language justice disproportionately impacts low-income immigrant parents' ability to advocate for their children" (p. 198).

Barriers for Somali Parent School Involvement

McBrien (2015) observed that "most teachers in the U.S. have not been prepared to teach and help refugee students" (p. 457). This finding is supported by an international study of the Somali refugee population in Sweden (Osman & Månsson, 2015) in which resettled Somali parents felt ill-equipped to navigate the school setting. The researchers examined "how Somali parents and Swedish teachers relate to each other and how the nature of the relationship impacts the school experience of [the Somali] children" (p. 37).

Specifically, the Swedish study asked, "What kind of obstacles do the parents encounter in supporting a proactive academic performance of their children [. . .]?" and "What types of social network are the Somali parents embedded in [that] affect their relation with the school teachers?" (p. 38). Based on the experiences of Somali parents, "the communication between the parents and the school or the teacher [was] exacerbated by the language barrier and the parents' limited educational experiences" (Osman & Månsson, 2015, p. 44).

Having another teacher function as an interpreter provided Somali parents with explanations about practices and procedures of the school in ways that they could better understand. Osman and Månsson (2015) stated, "More importantly, the parents felt that they could present their case and make their voices heard in their own language" (p. 45).

Acculturation

Early definitions of acculturation included "a process of adaptation to new conditions of life" (Thurnwald, 1932, p. 557), and the "processes whereby the culture of a society is modified as the result of contact with the culture of one or more other societies" (Gillin & Raimy, 1940, p. 371). Simply put, Berry (2005) said acculturation is "living successfully in two cultures" (p. 697).

More specifically he stated, "Acculturation is the dual process of cultural and psychological change that takes place as a result of contact between two or more cultural groups and their individual members" (p. 698). Speaking to the process of acculturation for refugees in general, McBrien (2005) stated, "At the individual level, changes can occur in one's sense of identity, values, and beliefs" (p. 330).

According to Isik-Ercan (2015), the issue of an individual being both Muslim and American is one of educational importance. The factors involved include recognition of religious diversity, lack of knowledge about Islam in American schools and society, and stereotypes fueled by political rhetoric (Isik-Ercan, 2015; Zine, 2000).

Isik-Ercan (2015) stated, "Being exposed to multiple discourses about culture, religion, and history through family, community and school interactions may compel immigrant children to be more conscious about many aspects of their identities" (p. 226). However, studies have found that although the degree to which adolescents assimilate can present its challenges, Muslim American students tend to not consider their bicultural or parallel identities to be a problem (Isik-Ercan, 2015; McBrien, 2005; Zine, 2000).

Assimilation

One early description of assimilation was the process in which one group incorporates the memories, sentiments, and attitudes of another group into a common cultural life (Park & Burgess, 1924). Bosswick and Heckman (2006) defined assimilation as a one-sided process of integration in which immigrants "disregard the values and practices of their countries of origin" (p. 7).

Drawing from Gordon's (1964) work on assimilation, Darboe (2003) examined the Somali resettled population in Minnesota. Darboe cited Gordon's *three major ideologies of assimilation*. These are Anglo-conformity (which proposes that racially minoritized people should adopt the cultural patterns of the dominant culture), the melting pot ideology (in which each group's culture and society mixes with the host's, creating a uniquely distinct culture and society), and cultural pluralism (implying that each racial group is allowed to express their own cultural and societal values without fear of discrimination) (Darboe, 2003; Gordon, 1964).

Implications from Darboe's (2003) work indicated a number of interesting factors. Among these were noted, "The subordinate group is [often] caught between two cultures and can never fully assimilate because they are dissimilar or rejected by the dominant group," "immigration and assimilation will continue to be a perennial concern for policy makers and governments because of wars, famine, and rapid population growth in developing countries," and "if economic conditions are good in the receiving country like the United States, immigrants are accepted and the opposite is true" (p. 469).

Most notably, the Minnesota study suggested that "Somalis are faced with more pressing social issues like learning the English language, and working and raising children in a different environment" (p. 469). Finally, Darboe indicated that in the years following 9/11, Somalis have been the targets of racial profiling.

METHODOLOGY

This study examines the way in which Somali Muslim parents perceive school-community relations. Specifically, the study was concerned with how these parents view the schools' efforts to connect with them through parental involvement opportunities and interactions with school leadership. Researchers utilized a researcher-developed questionnaire protocol designed to provide open-ended questions to prompt participants to elaborate and share stories about their perceptions of school-community relations regarding their children's education. This included ways in which they make meaning of parental involvement, interactions with administration and teachers, and their experience of school culture.

Sample

Using purposeful sampling, families were selected from school districts in a major Midwest urban setting that serve one of the largest resettled Somali Muslim communities in the Midwestern United States (Kallick & Mathema, 2016). The twelve participants (four women and eight men with a combined number of fifty-six children) in the study were adults (eighteen years or older), parents originally from Somalia with school-age children enrolled in urban K-12 schools in a Midwest urban area (see table 5.1).

Purposeful sampling was used due to the study's focus on an in-depth understanding of specific circumstances or phenomena (Patton, 2015). As Patton stated, "Information-rich cases are those from which one can learn a

Table 5.1 Participants

Name	Gender	Year Arrived in the United States	Number of Children	Grade Level/Status of Students
Absame	Male/Father	1999	3	5th grade, 3rd grade, kindergarten
Buule	Male/Father	1996	3	3rd grade, 2nd grade, pre-K
Beydan	Female/Mother	1998	5	6th grade, 3rd grade, 1st grade, 2 in college
Hodan	Female/Mother	1994	5	9th grade, 8th grade, 5th grade, 3rd grade, 1st grade
Jamilah	Female/Mother	1995	7	1 in college, 3 in high school, 2 in middle school, 1 in elementary
Mohmed	Male/Father	1997	4	1 in high school, 8th grade, 5th grade, 4th grade
Maajid	Male/Father	1996	3	3rd grade, 2nd grade, pre-K
Mahmoud	Male/Father	2000	6	6th grade, 5th grade, 2nd grade, kindergarten, pre-K, preschool
Marshud	Male/Father	2000	3	3rd grade, kindergarten, special needs program
Muumin	Male/Father	1999	2	kindergarten, preschool
Muusee	Male/Father	1997	6	8th grade, 7th grade, 5th grade, 4th grade, 3rd grade, 2nd grade, 1st grade
Sahra	Female/Mother	1995	9	2 college graduates, 1 in college, 1 high school senior, 3 in middle school, 2 in elementary

great deal about issues of central importance to the purpose of the research" (p. 53).

Purposeful sampling allows for participants to be selected on the basis of their ability to inform a specific topic or case. While the participants were current or former members of a single resettled community, they represented several school zones within one urban area. The participants in this area were selected due to being one of the largest resettled Somali communities in the United States.

Interview

The study utilized a semi-structured interview protocol to uncover thematic units based on emergent patterns of parent experiences and perceptions, as well as the understanding of concepts about their views of parent involvement, school-community relations, and school administration. Qualitative interviewing seeks to make meaning and provide in-depth understanding, especially to underrepresented populations (Denzin & Lincoln, 2011; Patton, 2015). Creswell (1998) stated that the "researcher seeks a collection of instances from data, hoping that issue-relevant meanings will emerge" (p. 154). This process allowed us to make direct interpretations.

Analysis

Glesne (1999) discussed a thick description as offering the qualitative researcher the opportunity to move beyond the mere act or behavior or phenomenon of the study (defined as thin description) to a more complete and complicated understanding of the totality of the experience. All interviews were transcribed verbatim and field notes were also used as a data source.

Researchers then entered transcriptions into Microsoft Excel, which served as an organizing medium, separating participant responses into cells, and labeling responses with initial codes that were subsequently grouped into code families (Saldaña, 2015). This process allowed researchers to sort responses by codes and identify patterns within responses that related to one another (Patton, 2015; Saldaña & Omasta, 2018).

Marshall and Rossman (1999) discussed this technique as noting patterns evident in the setting and expressed by participants. These patterns and themes served as a starting point to analyze and assess the central research questions stated earlier in this research. Specifically, as Rubin and Rubin (2005) stated, this means arranging the data into "topical markers" that allowed us to "combine what different interviewees have said about the same concepts" (p. 224).

The researchers' reflexivity was a reported process of interpretation. As a result, emergent data and categorical themes as the primary vehicle for presentation and analysis was utilized. Moreover, methods of validation and trustworthiness included thick rich description, inter-rater reliability, reflexivity, and researcher background. Specifically, inter-rater reliability consisted of all six research members coding transcriptions independently and then comparing codes in a group setting with all team members present.

The research team consisted of individuals with backgrounds in educational leadership, counselor education, and teacher education. In addition, the team included a research member with knowledge and connections to Somali Muslim language and culture, as well as her own experiences as a resettled individual.

Ethical Considerations

The study received Institutional Review Board approval, and researchers obtained informed consent from participants prior to conducting interviews. Interviews were conducted at a site chosen by the participants, and all participants were given the option to discontinue the interviews at any point. In addition, the researchers remained sensitive to social and cultural norms of the participants. Participants were given the opportunity to choose the location where and times when the interviews would be conducted and were explained the nature of the study and provided consent before taking part in the interviews.

Specifically, it was important that one of the collaborators was from the community and a native Somali/Arabic speaker. With one of the coinvestigators being of Somali origin and familiar with customs and expectations of the participants, she was able to conduct interviews with non-English speakers or those with limited English language skills. Additionally, she aided the team in ensuring the participants were made to feel secure and comfortable.

FINDINGS

The research questions for this study examined the perceptions of Somali Muslim refugee parents regarding the expectations they have for the education of their children, and the ways in which resettled Somali Muslim parents describe their experiences with the education of their children in urban schools. The researchers identified four themes relating to these concepts by examining and reexamining the data for useful patterns and participant responses that provide evidence of themes and issues.

The themes that emerged were: being Somali, becoming American; school choice; parental concerns ("I Do Have Fear"); and mitigating peer influences. The theme being Somali, becoming American deals with issues of acculturation and assimilation and speaks directly to parent expectations for their children's education. School choice and parental concerns deals with the manner in which they have experienced firsthand, in their own words, the education of their children. Mitigating peer influences is a theme that concerns both expectations and experiences.

Being Somali, Becoming American

Integration or acculturation was a major concern. Consistently participants voiced a significant amount of preoccupation with maintaining their identity as Somali while simultaneously speaking of a desire to be accepted as "Americans." While participants did not view this commitment to their heritage, culture, and religion as a problem, they perceived that non-Somali, non-Islamic groups might not understand. As one participant stated,

> We consider ourselves Somali Americans. We are American now. I mean my kid will be here.... I mean they're first generation [Americans]. They were born here. They're growing up here. They watch American TV. They like American people. So they will be in the melting pot, or what[ever] they call it. But still their father is originally from Somalia.

Another participant made an interesting distinction between assimilation and integration, stating,

> I mean you cannot be outsider. I mean you can still [be] active, integrate, but don't lose your identity. So there are two things that they will need to know: integration and assimilation. I mean integration means that you are acting with everybody—you are working with everybody—doing the same thing that they are doing. But you are not assimilated and do whatever they do for their life. So that's the difference between integration and assimilation.

For this participant, the importance of this distinction focused on not merely the social well-being of the child but indicated a critical concern with maintaining the child's identity as Somali and Muslim. This parent went on to add,

> I want my child to be active in the school environment, to do whatever the other kids are doing in the school, community wise, social wise, contribution wise, activities that I was doing when I was in college. So that's even what I want him to do.

This emphasized the significance of socializing and participating with others, but not necessarily appropriating the identity or culture of their "American" peers. Parents wanted their children to experience life and be exposed to academic and cultural knowledge yet not sacrifice their religious and cultural selves. As noted in a recent National Public Radio segment of *Morning Edition*, Muslim parents are seeking an education that "cultivates and nurtures a thriving American Muslim identity that balances religious, academic and cultural knowledge and imparts the importance of civic involvement and charitable work" (Al-Fatih Academy, n.d.; National Public Radio, 2017).

School Choice

A distinction should be made that while in most states charters are considered public schools, in some states charter schools are designated chartered *nonpublic* schools (Ohio Department of Education, 2018a). As well, as Brown (2015) pointed out,

> Charter school critics argue that charters amount to a privatization of public schools because they are run by organizations that don't answer to the public and in some states aren't subject to key rules that apply to government agencies, such as open meetings and public records laws. (Para. 4)

This distinction is particularly relevant to this study and to the manner in which parent participants defined school choice.

All participants, to some degree, talked about their choice of schools. Many had opted to take their children out of the traditional city schools and place them in charter schools. Others had moved to suburban districts to be closer to alternatives in community schools that were in their opinion more inclusive and responsive to their needs as Muslims and Somalis.

As one parent informed, "Public schools in this area are not the greatest places. You want, at the end of the day, [to] send your child to learn something, you know, to be someone tomorrow." This parent told us that parents rarely enroll younger, early childhood students in traditional, non-charter public school. In her words, "To be honest with you, most of the people that I meet either go to charter school or private school."

Predominantly, participants indicated that while they themselves finished their education in traditional public schools, they have determined to give their children an alternative. As another participant said,

> As [a] parent I wanted my kids to be educated and get the opportunity for education that many people don't have it in the world we come from, Somalia. So that's [the] opportunity for us to see our kids educated and grow up as people who are educated. [I]f you're in [the large urban district], and you also have charter schools in [the large city district], those also come from under the umbrella of the [City] Public Schools. So, in that case, even though now my kids

are going to private school—like a charter school—at the same time they still fall under the criteria of the [City] Public Schools district.

Participants also elaborated on the various personal reasons why they choose alternative or community schools instead of traditional P-12 public schools. Among these were religious convictions. As one male participant explained, in his opinion, nontraditional charter schools tended to be more sensitive to the nuances of Muslim values. In his words,

> There are a lot of things that Muslims believe in terms of the oneness of God or who God is, and sometimes, going through the curriculum, you're learning several gods here. Zeus is a god. The kid comes home talking about some random idol that is God. So sometimes in the curriculum, even going through the different curriculums, there are certain things that are sensitive within our culture.

Also, this father mentioned that Somali parents often go to school asking that their children not be involved in health education classes relating to sex education. As a culturally sensitive issue as well as a religious concern, Muslim Somali individuals see this as a parental responsibility.

As he informed us, "Parents say, no, I'll teach my kid what is moral and what is right when the time comes. I don't want you showing them certain things. Because culturally sensitive and, especially from a religious perspective." While this statement focused more on sex education in schools, content taught in general curriculum and culturally bound issues also factor into school choice. Discussing experiences with his own child in kindergarten, he stated in a matter-of-fact tone,

> I understand how a lot of activities—learning activities—if you're studying the letter V and it's Valentine's, it's St. Valentine's Day, or Halloween or even at Christmas season . . . conflict in many ways? . . . I think it's cultural, not religious.

From his dialogue, the complexities of the contributing factors that lead to Somali families choosing charter and community schools instead of the local public schools were recognized. Schools in American society have normalized or at the least secularized certain aspects of Judeo-Christian religion in schools. While many educators view these as a matter of teaching culture, this coupling of religious-secular aspects in U.S. curricula create concerns for Muslim Somali families that are committed to their own set of traditions and values. He continued,

> If you really look at it, it is coming from a religion perspective, such as Valentine [and] Christmas, and kids go through that experience. Some parents might

have a concern about it, but sometimes they talk to their children and explain to them, "This is what these people believe; this is what we believe."

This comment elucidates the complicated dynamics that Somali parents have to negotiate when their children participate in many activities of public schools. The participants in this study desired to send their children to schools that recognized and respected the aspirations they had for their children as well as validated their value system as Muslims. Although participants often opted out of traditional public schools, this did not diminish the value that they placed on education. As one female participant put it,

> Education is very important. . . . We're very educated, very well, . . . even though there are some myths that people may have that Muslims are non-educated, especially the girls [. . .]. I have two girls and three boys, so I want them [to have] the same, to be educated and pursue what they want to do for their lives. So education is really very important for us, I mean as Somali community, even though I have seen with my own eyes that parents who cannot even read and write, you see everybody taking their kids to the library. You see them pushing that. You see them doing that even though the father cannot read or the mother cannot read. So that tells you how they value education.

In this regard, school choice represented a major concern for Somali Muslim parents. By having "a say" in where their children attended school and being able to select a school sensitive to their needs, parents felt connected and able to maintain a feeling of belonging to the school community while still being who they perceived themselves to be. This also fostered in them an already existing appreciation of education.

Quotes such as this latter one implied that some parents might have felt disconnected or "unwelcomed" in schools due to their own lack of education—concerned with how they thought it would potentially be seen by teachers or school leaders. However, this lack of feeling a part of the school community had no bearing on the value they placed on the education of their children. By enrolling their children in school where they did feel connected fostered in them a sense of empowerment and involvement.

Parental Concerns ("I do have fear")

Wingfield and Karaman (2002) stated, "Despite the multicultural philosophy that currently prevails in American education, ADC [American-Arab Anti-Discrimination Committee] has found many teachers and the public at large not yet sufficiently sensitized to the problem of anti-Arab and anti-Muslim stereotyping" (p. 134). Various participants among Somali parents confirmed lack of sensitivity. They exhibited unique and at sometimes complex concerns about stereotyping, bias, and other forms of injustices.

Specifically, one Somali mother revealed a fear of how her child would be treated based on his name and his appearance. With some degree of anxiety, she noted,

> I fear . . . I honestly do have a fear. My son, he's 13, [and] he's very tall. He's 6'2". Usually [he] looks like he's older than his age, and I have so much fear that when they see his name, if they see him as covered in this (gestured to his hoodie), I ask, what can happen tomorrow? I have fear from the police, to be honest with you.

In this case, the participant clarified that she was speaking about the school, specifically the administration. She noted,

> I fear that sometimes the [school] administration is [biased]. If anything goes wrong, can other kids or white kids get away with it? My son cannot get away with it simply because of his name and his face. So, of course, yeah, I do have fear. Honestly, I'm a mother so mothers always [are] more concerned than fathers. At the same time, the fact is we can't be blind, [that's] the fact. I have so much fear that what had happened to him is just what happens. So yes, I do have a fear.

Another participant spoke specifically of the fear she had of her daughters being bullied due to their dress. She stated,

> For example, I have nine children. Six of them, they are girls. They wear [a] hijab scarf. They [are] really young and when they used to go to public schools, they had more bothering [bullying] from the other kids. Why you worrying? Why you covering up? Why you wear this? Why you that way? They called them names and always wanted [to bother them], and I never put my children on the school bus because they always were having difficulty, difficulty, difficulty.

Mitigating Peer Influence

A final theme that emerged from the study dealt with how parents handled an overarching preoccupation with the issue of peer influence. In many ways this theme connected the previous three themes. The data revealed that the worry Somali parents had that peers would have a negative influence on the academic and social lives of their children was a cause for enrolling them in nontraditional schools.

Additionally, the need to mitigate peer influence shared certain elements with the earlier themes of parental concerns and becoming American, being

Somali. However, in the context of the interviews mitigating peer influences on their children's school, experiences stood out as an independent and unique problem that parents felt a need to address.

Somali parents recognized that cultural influence—particularly in regard to peers—is a complex issue. In the words of one parent,

> This is, I think normal, because I think the American culture, [that is] the Caucasian-American culture, is the predominant social norms. That culture is one that [has] the predominance over others. Nobody can help. That would be something that is natural, but sometimes the student body would also have to be, you know, considered when teaching stuff, when designing material, when meeting with parents. So culture and diversity would have be part of how things are done.

Related to school environments created by peer influences another parent participant noted,

> The most worrying thing is the students, obviously. It's the environment that they go in. You want your kid to be in a good environment, to have good influences, to challenge themselves. But at the same time, one of the hardest things is—and I have to deal with it—is being a little bit different in terms of culture, in terms of maybe religion, in terms of all of that, and to have to kind of teach myself to be part of that group. Because, as a young kid, as you can understand, you have to be part of that system, whatever you are.

For many participants the complex nature of their children's school environments creates real dilemmas related to preserving and protecting their cultural expectations for education. Specifically, participants discussed the social dimensions of being in traditional Westernized public spaces where certain components of adolescent behavior conflict with traditional Somali cultural expectations. For example as one participant stated,

> I'd rather take them to home school than take my children there [in an urban public school], because it's just not a good school. I mean when I say that it's not a good school, at my high school people were smoking weed on the stairs.

This father continued noting that charter schools were a viable alternative to his children's public school experiences,

> So those are the areas [peer pressure, drugs, sex] that many parents thought, and some communities thought that they might need some kind of institution that can cater [to] their needs. So that's why charter schools came into place, to provide that need that community specifically may have, like Somali community.

Another participant expressed a deep concern for sending his children to traditional public schools stating,

> When you know you got to send [your kid] to a place [public schools] that he might be influenced in a wrong way, then obviously your child is just going somewhere to pick up from the bad habits. [. . .] And it's not like I want to generalize people, but the fact of the matter is, you know, I've seen it first hand. A lot of times public schools are pretty tough, especially in [urban schools], especially in certain areas.

This participant voiced a concern about a certain school as "a gang-infested place" due to his personal experiences as a student there. He went on to add, "I remember one day we took a cab from downtown and we wanted to come here, and we give him the address, and he dropped us pretty much a mile from here." In his perception, the cab driver's reluctance to enter the neighborhood was representative of how people viewed the condition of area and the schools there. As with most parents, the participants wanted their children to be educated without fear of being negatively influenced or mistreated.

DISCUSSION

The participants of this study offer important insights for traditional, non-charter public education leaders that specifically relate to the perceptions and experiences of Somali refugee parents with public education. In particular the findings answer the questions of (1) the perceptions of Somali Muslim refugee parents regarding their expectations of the education of their children and (2) how resettled Somali Muslim parents experience the education of their children in multiple school districts of an urban setting.

These findings were reported through the themes of being Somali, becoming American (which concerns assimilation and acculturation), school choice, parental concerns (which addressed parent fears and perceptions of non-charter public schools), and mitigating peer influences of their school-age children. The following discussion synthesizes those themes in relations to the research questions.

The importance Somali refugee parents' place on education and educational obtainment is document in the literature (Isik-Ercan, 2015). This emphasis seems to place Somali parents in position of trying to manage the complexities of cultural expectations and their children's assimilation into the perceived negative peer culture of the United States. Specifically, the behavior of other students in public schools was a primary parental concern. This was likely due to a sense of losing control over their identity and the way in which they hope to raise their children.

For these parents they feel that they can exercise the most control in the area of educational choice. Specifically, nine of the twelve participants in this study had made the decision to move their children to charter or private schools. The reality of this study's participants deciding to move away from public education is profound, especially in terms of the potential economic impact on a single school district.

Revenues into school districts are typically based on statewide formulas that take into consideration the enrollment/attendance of students. State policies often target funding for particular student populations, for example, children designated as second language learners or as economically disadvantaged (Chingos & Blagg, 2017).

Therefore, state expenditures translate to revenue for school districts in terms of instructional and pupil support (Ohio Department of Education, 2018b). Given this consideration, it could be calculated that based on a 2014 public school operating spending of $11,000 dollars per student for the city school district in the area of this study, participants have the potential to generate an estimated loss of $500,000 dollars per year in revenue by removing their fifty-one children from the traditional public education system (Ohio Legislative Service Commission, 2018).

Closely connected to school choice and an important finding of this work is the fear many participants expressed regarding the treatment of their children and exposure to cultural elements in public spaces including public schools. Parents wanted to know their children were safe and that the values of their family were respected.

Based on the findings, there seemed to be a degree of mistrust from certain parents for authorities (i.e., school administrators) that echoed the current racial and religious discrimination in society. While this finding emerged as the perception of the participating parents, there is also evidence for this concern in the literature (Ghaffari & Çiftçi, 2012; Haddad, 2004; Waters & Eschbach, 1995). At least one parent emphatically voiced a concern that her children would be misidentified with other students that she perceived were negatively treated by people in authority.

School-family communication was another issue of concern for Somali parents. Several parents referenced the way in which one district provided information on their website in their home language and providing translators for parents at the school. For these individuals this was not only a concern of language justice but also a way to acknowledge their culture and make them feel welcome. Teacher communication in one-on-one conferences and interactions also emerged as an immediate concern for several parents. While some participants referenced school-to-parent communication as a concern, data suggested a general feeling of being dismissed. An exemplar quote offered from one participant was,

> I don't think [the city] public school system was very much looking forward to or was very much interested in parental involvement in the kids. I don't know the reasons. The reasons could be primarily the fact that they have a general misperception about parents as being uneducated, as being not able to speak the language, and therefore they're not probably invested in interacting with them. Or it could be just the fact that we're grouped together with the larger black community, which is not very much received by the school system.

While this perception is recognized as a possible factor of the language barrier (possibly resulting from a lack of translators on the part of the school and a lack of fluency for parents), this is viewed as a relevant concern that warrants the attention of school leaders and teachers.

CONCLUSION

In closing, the following three recommendations could help educational leaders in public schools better serve the needs and exceptions of Somali refugee families. Based on the findings of this study, it is recommended that public school educational leaders:

1. be mindful of the cultural, linguistic, and religious diversity of resettled (as well as other immigrant) students in their schools and implement policies that are sensitive to these differences;
2. foster democratic spaces in their schools for conversations to discuss socially and culturally diverse concerns and to examine commonalities of concerns from parents from different sociocultural backgrounds; and
3. promote opportunities at the classroom level for teachers and parents of varying linguistic and cultural backgrounds to communicate with one another and prepare school personnel to employ culturally relevant practices.

In considering these recommendations, public education leaders and legislators should reflect on the ramifications of implementing various practical solutions. Specifically, school administrators and policymakers can remain open to their role as democratic agents. This includes being conscience of the rights and responsibilities of parents and communities that their schools serve, especially relating to resettled families and their needs.

By offering professional development opportunities for educators and educational leaders to become more proficient in strategies to communicate with parents and community members of varying linguistic and cultural backgrounds would be one example. Also, educational leaders can create parent-teacher programs to involve and educate all stakeholders. An example of this would be offering trainings for classroom teachers to develop their communication skills with non-English or culturally diverse populations.

Finally, it is important to seek out community advocates to help improve understanding the culture and customs of resettled populations and initiating proactive relationship building. In particular these practices should align with the academic and social needs of resettled (and immigrant) students in their schools.

If these recommendations are implemented, educational administrators and other public school educators will begin to foster innovative ways of making schools more socially just and culturally relevant for resettled and immigrant populations. Through democratic dialogue educational leaders can create spaces for community stakeholders to engage in meaningful, respectful discussion that will lead to a better understanding of diverse cultures. In doing so, the hope is that schools would develop welcoming multicultural climates for Somali parents and other parents of students from resettled and immigrant communities.

REFERENCES

Ahmad, I., & Szpara, M. Y. (2003). Muslim children in urban America: The New York City schools experience. *Journal of Muslim Minority Affairs, 233*, 295–301.

Al-Fatih Academy. (n.d.). Vision & mission. Retrieved April 20, 2017, from http://www.alfatih.org/about-us/vision_mission.cfm.

Bond, L., Giddens, A., Cosentino, A., Cook, M., Hoban, P., Haynes, A., Scaffidi, L., Dimovski, M., Cini, E., & Glover, S. (2007). Changing cultures: Enhancing mental health and wellbeing of refugee youth people through education and training. *Promotion & Education, 14*(3), 143–149.

Bosswick, W., & Heckman, F. (2006). *Integration of migrants: Contribution of local and regional authorities*. Dublin, IR: European Foundation for the Improvement of Living and Working Conditions.

Brown, E. (February 4, 2015). Are charter schools public or private? *The Washington Post*. Retrieved from https://www.washingtonpost.com/news/local/wp/2015/02/04/are-charter-schools-public-or-private/?noredirect=on&utm_term=.a361043e63d3.

Carlock, R. (2014). Parents, organized: Creating conditions for low-income immigrant parent engagement in public schools. In P. C. Gorski & J. Landsman (Eds.), *The poverty and education reader: A call for equity in many voices* (pp. 195–206). Sterling, VA: Stylus.

Chingos, M. M., & Blagg, K. (2017). *Making sense of state school funding policy*. Washington, DC: The Urban Institute.

Correa-Velez, I., Gifford, S. M., & Barnett, A. G. (2010). Longing to belong: Social inclusion and wellbeing among youth with refugee backgrounds in the first three years in Melbourne, Australia. *Social Science & Medicine, 71*(8), 1399–1408.

Creswell, J. W. (1998). *Qualitative inquiry and research design: Choosing among five traditions.* Thousand Oaks, CA: Sage.

Darboe, K. (2003). New immigrants in Minnesota: The Somali immigration and assimilation. *Journal of Developing Societies, 19*(4), 458–472.

Denzin, N. K., & Lincoln, Y. S. (2011). Introduction: The discipline and practice of qualitative research. In N. K. Denzin & Y. S. Lincoln (Eds.), *The Sage handbook of qualitative research* (4th ed., pp. 1–19). Los Angeles, CA: Sage.

Fagen, P. W. (2011). *Refugees and IDPs after conflict: Why they do not go home* (Special Report 268). Washington, DC: United States Institute of Peace.

Ghaffari, A., & Çiftçi, A. (2012). Religiosity and self-esteem of Muslim immigrants to the United States: The moderating role of perceived discrimination. *The International Journal for the Psychology of Religion, 20*(1), 14–25.

Gillin, J., & Raimy, V. (1940). Acculturation and personality. *American Sociological Review, 5*, 371–380.

Glesne, C. (2006). *Becoming qualitative researchers: An introduction* (4th ed.). Boston, MA: Pearson/Allyn and Bacon.

Gordon, M. M. (1964). *Assimilation in American life.* New York, NY: Oxford University.

Guo, Y. (2011). Perspectives of immigrant Muslim parents: Advocating for religious diversity in Canadian schools. *Multicultural Education, 18*(2), 55–60.

Haddad, Y. Y. (2004). *Not quite American? The shaping of Arab and Muslim identity in the United States.* Waco, TX: Baylor University Press.

Huddleston, T., & Wolffhardt, A. (2016). *Back to school: Responding to the needs of newcomer refugee youth.* Brussels, BE: Migration Policy Group.

Isik-Ercan, Z. (2015). Being Muslim and American: Turkish-American children negotiating their religious identities in school settings. *Race, Ethnicity and Education, 18*(2), 225–250.

Jeynes, W. H. (2003). A meta-analysis: The effects of parental involvement on minority children's academic achievement. *Education & Urban Society, 35*(2), 202–218.

Kallick, D. D., & Mathema, S. (2016). *Refugee integration in the United States.* Washington, DC: Center for American Progress.

Marshall, C., & Rossman, G. B. (1999). *Designing qualitative research.* Thousand Oaks, CA: Sage.

McBrien, J. L. (2005). Educational needs and barriers for refugee students in the United States: A review of the literature. *Review of the Educational Research, 75*(2), 329–364.

McBrien, J. L. (2015). Serving the needs of at-risk refugee youth: A program evaluation. *Journal of School Public Relations, 36*(4), 444–62.

McCreery, E., Jones, L., & Holmes, R. (2007). Why do Muslim parents want Muslim schools? *Early Years, 27*(3), 203–19.

Nadeau, P. (2008). *The Lewiston Somalis: Current and future workforce development challenges.* Lewiston, ME: Center for Workforce Research and Information, Maine Department of Labor and Maine State Planning Office.

National Public Radio. (2017). *This Islamic school teaches how to be Muslim, and American* [Video file]. Retrieved June 8, 2017, from http://www.npr.org/.

Nezer, M. (2013). *Resettlement at risk: Meeting emerging challenges to refugee resettlement in local communities*. Silver Spring, MD: HIAS.

Noguera, P. A. (2004). Social capital and the education of immigrant students: Categories and generalizations. *Sociology of Education, 77*(2), 180–83.

Ohio Department of Education. (2018a). Chartered nonpublic school information. Retrieved from http://education.ohio.gov/Topics/Quality-School-Choice/Private-Schools/Chartered-Nonpublic-School-Information.

Ohio Department of Education. (2018b). Expenditure per pupil rankings. Retrieved from http://education.ohio.gov/Topics/Finance-and-Funding/Finance-Related-Data/Expenditure-and-Revenue/Expenditure-Per-Pupil-Rankings.

Ohio Legislative Service Commission. (2018). 2017 spending by county. Retrieved from https://www.lsc.ohio.gov/pages/budget/documents/statespendingbycounty.aspx?Year=2017.

Osman, A., & Månsson, N. (2015). "I go to teacher conferences, but I do not understand what the teacher is saying": Somali parents' perception of the Swedish school. *International Journal of Multicultural Education, 17*(2), 36–52.

Park, R. E., & Burgess, E. W. (1924). Assimilation. In *Introduction to the science of sociology* (pp. 734–783). Chicago, IL: University of Chicago Press.

Parker-Jenkins, M. (1991). Muslim matters: The educational needs of the Muslim child. *Journal of Ethnic and Migration Studies, 17*(4), 569–582.

Patton, M. Q. (2015). *Qualitative research and evaluation methods* (4th ed.). Thousand Oaks, CA: Sage.

Putnam, D. B., & Noor, M. C. (1993). *The Somalis: Their history and culture*. Washington, DC: Refugee Service Center, Center for Applied Linguistics.

Robinson, D., & Mazid, I. (2016). Embracing family diversity through transformative educational leadership, the ethics of care, and community uplift in schools. *Journal of School Public Relations, 37*(2), 203–26.

Rubin, H. J., & Rubin, I. S. (2012). *Qualitative interviewing: The art of hearing data* (3rd ed.). Thousand Oaks, CA: Sage.

Saldaña, J. (2016). *The coding manual for qualitative researchers* (3rd ed.). Thousand Oaks, CA: Sage.

Segal, U. A., & Mayadas, N. S. (2005). Assessment of issues facing immigrant and refugee families. *Child Welfare League of America, 84*(5), 563–83.

Saldaña, J., & Omasta, M. (2018). *Qualitative research: Analyzing life*. Thousand Oaks, CA: Sage.

Swarns, R. L. (2003). U.S. a place of miracles for Somali refugees. *New York Times*. Retrieved July 20, 2003, from http://www.nytimes.com/2003/07/20/us/us-a-place-of-miracles-for-somali-refugees.html.

Thurnwald, R. (1932). The psychology of acculturation. *American Anthropologist, 34*, 557–69.

Waters, M. C., & Eschbach, K. (1995). Immigration and ethnic and racial inequality in the United States. *Annual Review of Sociology, 21*, 419–46.

Wingfield, M., & Karaman, B. (2002). Arab stereotypes and American educators. In E. Lee, D. Menkart, & M. Okazawa-Rey (Eds.), *Beyond heroes and holidays: A practical guide to K-12 multicultural, anti-racist education and staff development* (pp. 132–36). Washington, DC: Network of Educators of Americas.

Zine, J. (2000). Redefining resistance: Towards an Islamic subculture in schools. *Race, Ethnicity and Education, 3*(3), 293–316.

Zinth, K. (2005). *Parental involvement in education.* Denver, CO: Education Commission of the States.

Chapter 6

Book Review

Partnering with Parents to Ask the Right Questions by Santana Luz, Dan Rothstein, and Agnes Bain

Art Stellar

Santana Luz, Dan Rothstein, and Agnes Bain. *Partnering with Parents to Ask the Right Questions* (Alexander, VA: ASCD, 2016), references, appendices, index, 234 pgs., softback, $29.95

Improving parental involvement is high on the agendas of many educators where parents have not participated in the past. They contend that parents do not know how to ask meaningful initial questions or follow-up questions that will enable them to understand the educational program and how to help their children.

This book is based upon the authors' experiences with parents and educators in Lawrence, Massachusetts, where all three of the authors live and work. All are also affiliated with the Right Question Institute which works across the country, developing an engagement strategy between parents and educators. They share a strong belief that many parents, especially minority parents, are too busy and uncomfortable in their interactions with school personnel to have meaningful dialogue.

Instead of presenting an overwhelming program that would cover all possible issues that might occur over the course of pre-K to 12 careers, the authors have narrowed their scope to a few points which they believe have the potential to address a multitude of occurrences. "Specifically, we have seen that strong partnerships emerge when parents learn to play three key roles effectively: They support their children's education at home, They monitor their progress, and They advocate for them when necessary" (p. 5).

Beginning as participants in a project to reduce the number of school dropouts, they found that parents were often stymied with asking educators about their children. The authors over time have developed a strategy for improving school-community relations based upon teaching parents how to ask the right questions; first in a workshop setting and then in a real situation.

The first approach, which they later abandoned, was to give parents lists of questions to ask educators. When parents kept asking for more questions, the authors realized that they had only succeeded in making the parents more dependent upon them. That is when over many trials and years of revisions, they evolved toward a system wherein parents learn to produce their own questions. They called this method the Question Formulation Technique (QFT).

Basically, this is how it works. Start with an issue or Question Focus (QFocus) which cannot be written in a question form. Next, usually in a small group setting, brainstorm as many questions as possible about the focus. In typical brainstorming fashion, questions are not debated or answered. Parents should be the ones generating the questions. After all the ideas are on the table, the group of parents should rewrite the questions to be more specific and more easily understood.

Ideally, there should be a mix of open and closed questions. Participants should then list the questions in priority order with initial questions and follow-up sub-questions. Parents should have the opportunity to reflect on the process. The goal is for parents to learn to ask better questions while they are becoming more comfortable with educators. Recognizing that schools usually lack resources for parental education, the authors suggest introducing the QFocus method repeatedly in different sessions over time. The idea is for educators to move from telling to asking. Parents should begin to ask more of their own questions which will raise their level of engagement.

Altogether, there are three tools presented. There is Support, Monitor, and Advocate; Framework for Accountable Decision-Making (FADM); and QFT.

FADM is relatively simple starting with the idea that a decision is when one selects one option from two or more options. If there is no choice, then no decision is necessary. There are "three basic criteria when looking at any decision-specially: The reasons for the decision, The process for making the decision, and The role of the person(s) affected by the decision in the decision-making process" (p. 100), There are three criteria to apply to decisions: there is a legitimate reason for the decision, there is a transparent process, and anyone affected by the decision has an opportunity to participate in the decision-making.

There is a chapter on using this process for school-initiated change, one on teacher-initiated change and other chapters for utilizing this process for changes around equity, English as a second language, and special education. Reading through each chapter is a bit redundant, but these later chapters can be a good resource for teachers and schools addressing those matters.

Appendix B: "Materials for facilitating the Right Question School-Family Partnership Strategy" is clearly the most useful part of this book and will likely be what practitioners—who adopt this approach—will utilize. This reviewer suggests xeroxing it to use as a lesson plan and modifying it to fit the local circumstances. This appendix includes "annotated facilitation guides for each one of the components of the strategy, handouts and worksheets for parents, and planning templates" (p. 181). It is suggested that the facilitator becomes totally familiar with this material before trying it out with a live audience.

While this book is useful, it is also very straightforward with little descriptive language to demonstrate real-life applications of the process. There is also no data to prove quantitatively or qualitatively that application of this process will improve results or enhance the efficiency for parents or educators. Nevertheless, it is intuitively safe to suggest that teaching parents how to ask questions will strengthen school-family partnerships when combined with other communications strategies.

To effectively implement the strategy outlined in this book is not expensive nor overly time consuming. There are no materials to purchase. While it might be a plus to have professional development activities for teachers and others prior to trying out these techniques, that is not required. Both the presenters and parents will gradually be able to move away from the outlines as they gain confidence with the materials. The authors believe that the mechanics contained in this book will over time transform the relationship between parents and educators. They feel that this may be the first step toward a real partnership.

According to the authors, "The actions in the case studies presented here demonstrates a willingness to share the power of the skills and an understanding that no one is 'giving up power' but, rather was sharing something powerful that could help them all to achieve common goals." "The professional and parents were modeling how to democratize access to skills that enable more effective action and stronger partnerships" (p. 174). Most educators will be in favor of expanding the capacity of parents to ask questions, although a few will not see the value until or unless it helps them do their jobs. Such is the nature of all partnerships.

Reviewed by Art Stellar, PhD, an assistant editor of the *Journal of Education Human Resources*, formerly *Journal of School Public Relations*.

Part II

HIGHER EDUCATION

Chapter 7

How Can Higher Education Engage with Rural Communities to Address Their Teacher Shortages?

Henry Tran and Theresa Harrison

INTRODUCTION

Higher education institutions (HEIs), since their inception, have been uniquely situated to address some of society's larger systemic issues through avenues such as educational attainment, workforce development, and technological advances. Yet, because universities and colleges are highly complex organizations, with multiple and sometimes competing missions, addressing societal concerns may not be a top priority.

The term "anchor institutions" was coined by Michael Porter in 2002 to describe entities, such as universities, with the potential to transform local communities and regions by investing their unique resources (Rutheiser, 2016). While each institution type (e.g., R1, community college) contributes toward its particular focus areas (e.g., research production, technical skill attainment), their geographic location may also exert influence on where institutional resources are invested.

Research efforts tend to be focused on the geographic region in which large universities are situated, which are often in urban areas. As such, there has been less scholarly work or policy attention on rural communities and their concerns (Cuervo, 2016). This is despite the fact that many rural communities face significant challenges that often match or surpass the level of severity in other geographic regions that receive more attention.

One major issue facing rural communities is the inadequate staffing of rural schools, as a result of their teacher recruitment and retention problems (Taie & Goldring, 2017; Tran, Smith, & Fox, 2018). For example, nationally, almost 40 percent of remote rural schools face severe teacher recruitment struggles, in every subject matter, with many of these vacancies caused by constant turnover, at a rate higher than other geographic locales (Malkus, Hoyer, & Sparks, 2015; Maranto & Schuls, 2012).

This results in these school employers facing disproportionately higher teacher replacement costs than their counterparts that do not share the same degree of teacher staffing problems (Barnes, Crowe, & Schaefer, 2008; Watlington, Shockley, Guglielmino, & Felsher, 2010). While the challenges may seem specific to schools, a systemic perspective is necessary to truly understand the rural teacher shortage crisis. HEIs play an important and unique role in that system to create a promising pathway of infusing new teachers into rural communities.

There are several challenges that prospective teachers must be willing to face, both personal and professional, to prepare them for work in a rural area. Prospective teachers are often dissuaded to work in rural schools because the geographic environments are routinely considered less desirable, with fewer amenities (such as shopping locations and entertainment), less job opportunities for their spouse and families, and lower pay (Hammer, Hughes, McClure, Reeves, & Salgado, 2005; Miller, 2008).

These issues are related to the fact that rural communities often have a lower tax base given that (a) fewer amenities and industry devalue the property in rural areas and (b) lower tax base means less tax revenue to pay public employees like teachers (Tran, 2018). It is important to note that regional variation in unemployment, poverty, and racial and cultural demographics add to the complexity of developing innovative solutions to some of these areas most challenging issues.

Additionally, it is unfortunately common in impoverished rural communities with frequent teacher shortages to see lower educational attainment of their youth and the associated lower economic standing of those students in their adulthood (Tran, 2018; Byun, Meece, & Irvin, 2012). These forces contribute to the dooming of the community to a vicious cycle of facing the same problems without redress given that the community will remain depressed. Consequently, it remains unattractive for prospective teachers to teach in those communities, which in turn hurt the educational and economic opportunities of the students, thereby repeating the cycle all over again. Figure 7.1 depicts this cycle.

The ability to provide quality education for the populace is multifaceted, requiring not only to have enough qualified teachers to meet the demand, but also to have teachers willing to serve wherever there is need, particularly in hard-to-staff rural areas. It has been suggested that HEIs can play a critical role in helping to alleviate rural teacher staffing problems (Cuervo, 2016; Tran, Smith, & Fox, 2018), but how that can be accomplished has not been thoroughly examined.

The mission of many HEIs, due to being either a land-grant university or their commitment to educating the citizenry of their state, foundationally

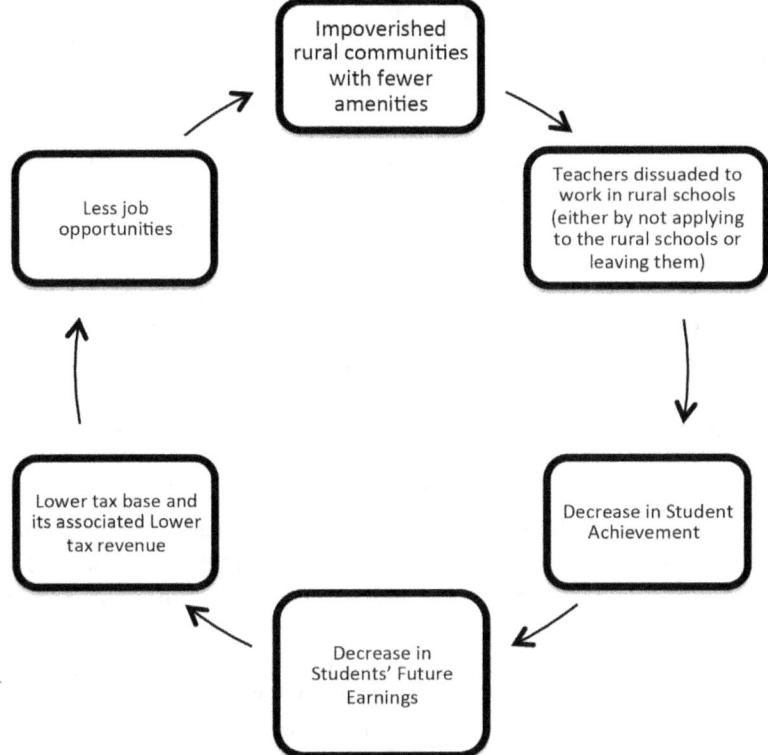

Figure 7.1   Cycle of Rural Impoverishment.

requires providing educational opportunities. Yet, the lack of investment, particularly in rural areas, by HEIs perpetuates rural teacher shortages. For example, the disconnect and lack of engagement between HEIs and rural communities is captured by the comparatively low representation of student teachers from rural areas enrolled at universities relative to other type of students, and the comparatively low proportion of student teachers placed in rural communities for their preservice field experience relative to other contexts (Maier & Youngs, 2009).

The inability to recruit and enroll a larger majority of in-state students from rural areas has long-term implications for both rural communities and HEIs alike. Rural communities are more likely to benefit from homegrown talent coming back to the community after degree completion. Therefore, HEIs must come to an understanding that placing regional interests at the forefront of their institutions' agenda is mutually beneficial. However, it requires taking a step outside of academia to engage local communities in conversations about shared interests and accomplishing shared goals.

Defining Community Engagement

The Carnegie Foundation defines community engagement as the "collaboration between institutions of higher education and their larger communities (local, regional/state, national, global) for the mutually beneficial exchange of knowledge and resources in a context of partnership and reciprocity" (Campus Compact, 2008). While HEIs can define what community engagement looks like for them, determining how it is enacted is often challenging.

For whom and for what purpose do HEIs exist? This is a perennial question asked about universities since their inception. However, the answer often depends on the timeframe, geographic region, institution type, and constituency that has been asked, which may be indicative of a larger problem within the field of higher education and HEIs ability to initiate, collaborate, or sustain engagement in local and regional communities.

It is likely that the burgeoning systemic issues that continue to plague rural communities might provide the tipping point to further engage and coalesce HEIs in community engagement efforts. Yet, while higher education as a sector has publicly acknowledged that it has an important public mission, there remains a gap between intention and practice.

To address rural engagement, university teacher preparation programs, for instance, should not only provide students with rural teaching experiences, but also provide opportunities to acclimate, learn about, engage with, and immerse in rural communities beyond the school site, given the importance of the community influence on rural teachers' lives (Tran, Smith, & Fox, 2018). This requires spending more time in rural settings engaging students in beyond the classroom experiential learning opportunities.

Finding or developing curricular and cocurricular experiences of relevance (e.g., attending a fall festival, volunteering in a tutoring or mentoring program, conducting informational interviews) allows prospective teachers to acclimate themselves and establish a meaningful connection to the community. Additionally, student placements in internships at rural schools help attract high-quality talent to those schools; teaching interns expand rural schools' capacity to offer support to students; and student interns help enhance the instructional intensity at rural schools through co-teaching models, all while immersing student teachers in field placements within a setting in which they can be mentored and learn the rural context.

Through these avenues, rural community engagement can be a viable mechanism to enhance progress toward addressing communal issues, such as mitigating rural teacher staffing shortages, thus furthering the mission of HEIs. Ultimately, it is in anchor institutions' best interest to engage locally and align their mission and strategic plans with regional priority concerns.

For example, a coordinated effort linking a community college, a regional industry, and policy to encourage employment growth benefits all parties involved and stands to increase the competitiveness of the area. Community colleges are exemplars of community engagement within HEIs, serving the socioeconomic and educational needs of its local population by providing workforce training and continuing education (Jacob, 2015).

Therefore, considering the reach community colleges have as the primary higher education service provider in many parts of rural America, the community college is well positioned to serve as a civic intermediary to not only increase interest into the education profession, but also to serve as a hub that brings together other community and state resources to solve the daunting problem of rural educator recruitment and retention (Tran, Smith, & Fox, 2018).

The challenges for HEIs in the twenty-first century is to reexamine the historical perspectives and missions of HEIs and perhaps bring those institutions that have traditionally left this work to community colleges to account for how they are serving their local and regional communities. Community engaged institutions invest in the work of seeking change for the betterment of the communities they serve and not just doing community service.

This must become more of a priority for HEIs or they will find their value to the larger community context dwindling. HEIs, like R1 universities, can play a significant yet unique role in this system and can provide support with addressing regional communal problems, such as rural teacher shortages. This is due in part to their focus on research and innovation, geographic location, and the extent of their financial resources.

Barriers and opportunities to university and community engagement. While the breadth of literature on the benefits of university-community partnerships and the need for more community engagement from HEIs is promising, for those interested in this work, there are also some pitfalls that need to be addressed. In most cases, where a university is located is going to be the principal beneficiary of its research output. As such, regions further removed from the university have a tendency to be skeptical of HEIs and investing additional public funds in research on campus.

To add insult to injury, funding agencies tend to preference partnerships that integrate colleges and universities due to their regulatory compliance and automated financial systems; as a result, this puts community agencies in a position to be dependent on the university for funds (Gass, 2005). While these dynamics may make university-community partnerships strenuous, there is a multitude of potential beneficial outcomes for both HEIs and rural communities if they can agree on a common agenda and pool their resources to meet regional challenges. This also makes a strong case for building partnerships with institutions within and outside a campus system in order to reach different regions of a state.

By investing in inter and intra-institutional projects to solve regional problems, a specific HEI does not need to be located in the rural community of focus, but can contribute in other ways to meeting partnership goals. This requires shifting the focus from what benefits the university first, to what is mutually beneficial for both university and community, to an even more radical stance for some HEIs of what benefits the community first.

Universities, in many respects, do not disseminate information and innovation processes in a way that regions can access them and take advantage of the intellectual capital in their state. Moreover, if research is not particularly relevant to the rural context in terms of practical usefulness, there is a missed opportunity. Faculty members from all disciplines need to have incentives for investing time and resources to tackle the challenge of relevance to regional issues.

Research (the creation of innovation) is currently scattered across separate centers located in all colleges, distributed throughout the campus. As such, the bureaucratic nature of the HEI makes it difficult for those unfamiliar with academia to seek partnerships. Utilizing a centrally located center for community engagement efforts provides a one-stop shop for outside entities to request assistance and be referred to appropriate departments across the campus.

Unfortunately, without providing community agencies the opportunity to voice their own concerns, universities are often unfamiliar with local or regional concerns as it relates to development needs or competitive advantages (Drabenstott, 2008). Aligning research interests and regional community needs requires a multi-sector approach, including those most familiar with the issues in rural settings, on a broad scale and actively listening to their proposed solutions to those problems.

What Can HEIs Do to Improve Rural Teacher Staffing?

In the report *The Perspectives of Potential and Current Rural Teachers for Rural Teacher Recruitment and Retention in South Carolina*, Tran, Smith, & Fox, 2018 make several recommendations that HEIs can employ to help improve teacher recruitment and retention in rural hard-to-staff schools. Although the recommendations were made to address issues in a specific state context, they likely have applicability to rural environments across the nation. The following section will expand upon each of the recommendations outlined in that report and provide additional recommendations of how HEIs can engage with rural communities to mitigate rural teacher staffing shortages. In addition, examples of model programs are provided that have been successfully implemented in rural settings.

Contextually relevant teacher preparation for rural schools. According to a report by American College Testing (ACT, 2014), the United States faces a projected 14 percent increase in the number of secondary teachers needed between 2010 and 2021. However, from 2010 to 2014, high school graduates expressing an interest in the teaching profession decreased by 16 percent (ACT, 2014). These issues are exacerbated for rural locales. The most commonly cited reason for this declining interest is the lack of support and professional development opportunities in remote rural environments and the associated feeling of social isolation (Lock et al., 2012).

Additionally, Barley and Brigham (2008) highlighted a distinct lack of rural-specific training for prospective teachers. In fact, research with preservice teachers has suggested that their lack of self-confidence in being able to teach poor rural students negatively affects their interest in teaching at rural schools (Tran, Moon, & Hogue, 2015). Therefore, in keeping with the Council of Chief State School Officers (2012) recommendations, clinically based preparation programs must provide relevant, well-planned experiences to prepare teacher candidates. This will require taking a critical look at the traditional curriculum of teacher preparation programs and finding ways to embed components that diversify preservice teachers' understanding of rural student populations.

One proposal suggests that success with rural teacher preparation can be achieved through not only tailoring teaching courses to meet the needs of regional and remote communities, but by allowing preservice teachers the opportunity to experience working in remote areas (Ramsey, 2000). The 2:1 co-teaching model provides possible solutions to the problems of finding adequate, quality teaching placements in predominantly rural public school settings. By partnering preservice teachers with current teachers, a mentorship relationship can develop and allow preservice teachers an opportunity to be incorporated fully into the classroom setting. Also, reducing the number of placements promises more selectivity in the already limited number of placements available in rural areas and thus may enhance the quality of those placements.

Furthermore, Corbett (2016) argues rural teacher preparation should move beyond vocational training to "support ways of thinking about teaching in rural contexts that are non-standard and that directly address persistent and pressing rural problems such as: population loss, resource industry restructuring, resource depletion, environmental and habitat degradation and land use policy" (p. 147). It is commonly known that teaching, especially in rural contexts, can be plagued by many issues deemed beyond the scope of an educator. In viewing these issues and concerns as cyclical, then the need and responsibility to address any one issue becomes clear. This provides further opportunity for collaboration between HEIs and schools to consider the context for partnering, not one of simply placing teachers in a community to educate, but to truly transform rural communities to work for the benefit of all who live there. This would help address the ability to retain teachers, hopefully reduce the out-migration, as well as revive the local community.

Improving access to contextually relevant rural teacher professional development. All teachers benefit from professional development, but Babione (2010) concluded that the key concerns for rural teachers are flexibility, continuity, collaboration, and opportunities for curriculum development. With this in mind, HEIs should consider how they could collaborate with K-12 schools to provide additional professional development opportunities that address the issues of concern for teachers and executive leadership.

Yet, collaborating is a two-way street. Warren and Peel (2005) argued that in order for rural school reform to take place, administrators must be willing to establish partnerships with colleges and universities and engage teachers in that work as well. Thus alluding back to the previously mentioned need for a centralized office to handle community agency requests for seeking assistance. If too many hoops and barriers are put in place in order to establish partnerships, then schools that need an investment from HEIs may forego making an initial request.

The literature provides suggestions for the ways in which current school-university partnerships have had mutually positive outcomes. For example, HEIs are in a unique position to provide professional development, including continual education for rural teacher educators. One way to demonstrate support and retain rural teacher educators in their current placement is to find a way to not only make those offerings accessible, but easily transferable into degree or certificate completion programs.

HEIs can accomplish this by ensuring access to university programs for already employed rural teachers and a willingness to tailor certification to meet their unique needs via the project and field-based practicums requirements (Mollenkopf, 2009). The ability of rural teachers to complete certification coursework may be the difference between staying or leaving their current place of employment (Knapczyk, Chapman, Rodes, & Chung, 2001), which may further burden the schools.

How courses are structured and when and where they are offered all affect the perceived accessibility by teachers. Additionally, rural schools tend to have limited professional development funds, so the cost of traveling to a university outside of a reasonable geographic boundary may be limited. As such, online platforms are becoming more popular with the evolution of new technologies to provide distance education and teleconferencing services (Johnson, 2004).

One particular program coordinated by a partnership between the North-East Florida Educational Consortium (NEFEC) and the University of North Florida (UNF) is a school-based professional learning series called Essential Three or e3 (Ohlson, Johnson, Shope, & Rivera, 2018). The primary concern is to determine instructional priorities, while also identifying how to support rural districts and school leaders to meet identified aims.

UNF faculty and the NEFEC team, with input from a team of teachers and school leaders, chose to focus on deeper knowledge, collaboration, and engagement as it relates to observation and evaluation of classroom instruction. This partnership demonstrates the value of having input from HEIs, community content experts such as a consortium, the teachers, and executive leadership, all working together from the development, implementation, and research stages to create programs and services that all member districts could benefit from.

Teacher educators are trained with the understanding that student learning needs are diverse and that teacher educator needs are just as diverse. There is no one-size-fits-all approach; therefore, the more programs are designed to account for teacher educator interests and needs, provides flexibility, as well as autonomy, the more likely the program is to be successful.

In providing rural leader support it becomes clear that flexibility will be required of all participating collaborators. HEIs must rethink how standards, certification, and course offerings can be met, while also considering what additional professional development offerings might be advantageous for teacher educators by working in collaboration with other community partners within the region.

Contextually relevant professional development for rural school leaders. Retention of quality rural teachers is intricately dependent upon the principal, his/her leadership tactics, and his/her relationships with staff members (Lock et al., 2012). As such the need to continuously develop rural leaders is paramount to the success of a rural education enterprise and HEIs can play a pivotal role in providing or facilitating those development opportunities.

Stakeholders have different expectations of leadership within their communities, therefore leaders must be cognizant of the various needs of institutions and have the skill sets to meet them (Institute for Educational Leadership, 2005). For example, rural teacher leaders need to understand the industry needs of not only their local community but also their regional needs in order to best maximize potential job placements for their students' postgraduation.

It has been suggested that one way to mitigate the effects of geographic location and hone rural leaders' skills is through ongoing networking experiences (e.g., mentor-mentee) with other school district leaders. Thus promoting collaboration through creating a venue for open dialogue and reflection to change daily practice and strengthen school improvement (Augustine-Shaw, 2016). The mentoring and induction program coordinated by the Kansas Educational Leadership Institute (KELI) offers new rural principals and superintendents assistance in developing knowledge, applying skills, and promoting meaningful discussion in their local context (Augustine-Shaw, 2016).

The first component of note in the program is that trained mentors contextualize, for new superintendents, the skills necessary to be successful in smaller, rural districts. By aligning veteran and new superintendents that are both familiar and working in rural contexts, the mentor-mentee relationship provides an unparalleled opportunity to share best practice with the knowledge and assurance that your mentor has been through what you are going through.

The second component is high-quality professional development through seminars focused on current topics that provide exposure to content experts, demonstrate application in similar settings, and provides valuable networking among peers focused on using the lens of school district administrators. This type of leadership development program could improve rural teacher staffing outcomes. The structured nature of professional development opportunities lessens the social isolation some rural leaders experience as well as provides support and resources that may not otherwise be available to those in executive leadership roles. Additionally, leaders are supported in their decision-making as they can look at an issue from a variety of lenses and have context for their responsibility as an executive leader to weigh their decisions carefully. The additional support provided to principals can help them better attract and retain teachers through their improved ability to provide better teacher support.

Using the KELI program as an aspirational model, it is possible to envision how HEIs might also play a role in existing professional development activities. As previously mentioned, it would be advantageous for more teacher education programs to embed issues and concerns of rural areas into the curriculum. One way this could be done is to partner with rural schools so that many of the professional development seminars offered at rural schools could be open to teacher educators. This would provide teacher educators an opportunity to learn directly from executive leadership and explore a rural school, while also providing rural leaders an opportunity to recruit.

Many school districts seek to recruit teachers by attending university job fairs, but if rural districts are not invited or do not feel they would be competitive in that venue it is another missed opportunity. Perhaps instead of expecting rural leaders to come to HEIs, HEIs should continue to explore ways to get teacher educators into rural areas through institutional outreach.

Community Development and Resource Support

School-community partnerships are formal and informal support systems of people or entities committed to meeting education goals for student achievement and postsecondary aspirations. This support includes allocation of material, social, and knowledge-based resources to name a few provided by local entities (e.g., businesses, non-profits, and universities) (Alleman, 2013). This definition encapsulates what the literature states are important in forming effective partnerships in rural communities.

Therefore, one has to take into consideration all invested parties, as well as consider how each group might best contribute to the ultimate end goal. For instance, while HEIs might be able to provide human and knowledge-based resources, the local faith community may be able to provide social support and businesses provide economic support. More specifically, relying on local community agencies may result in long-term partnerships with multiple agencies.

With this in mind, there is a rural advantage in terms of a specific place-based culture with which to tie common goals that can propel a community toward success. The importance of highlighting these rural advantages as well as providing these resources and supports have been found to be important for teacher acclimation to the rural school context and their retention (Tran, Smith, & Fox, 2018).

Petrin, Schafft, and Meece (2012) found that local economic context, rather than the direct influence of educators, contributed most to the out-migration of rural youth. If rural youth do not see opportunities available to them and are encouraged by their parents to leave the rural community, the only way to combat this reason for out-migration is to find ways to build up the economic vitality of a rural region. This in turn will create a more favorable context for rural teacher attraction and the success of the local economy.

Ultimately, institutions must prioritize engaged scholarship and play an active role by providing incentives for faculty to conduct research and collaborate with industry on issues of relevance to rural regional areas. While service has long been advocated for as the third leg of tenure and promotion decisions and seen as a way to incentivize more faculty to engage in community engagement efforts, its elevation has not risen to the same level as research and teaching.

Perhaps using an economic engagement lens to align university and community leaders' interests will provide a common target with which to prioritize efforts. The following recommendations pulls from a variety of models that aim to achieve a true partnership by forming a network of key players within a region that are focused on addressing a common issue of concern.

Recommendations

A multi-sector approach to engagement as it relates to research and development opportunities seem to be the prevailing notion in the literature for how to galvanize existing community groups to work on a common issue.

First, when considering the role that HEIs can play in working among one another, there is a need to cultivate a spirit of shared success, not competition among research institutions. Second, a central mission of HEIs is knowledge production, which can be enhanced when multiple institutions are working together on a common agenda. Last but not least, the significance of community engagement as scholarship is recognizing that the ivory tower is not the keeper of all knowledge and that there is a lot to learn from community partners (Fitzgerald, 2012).

Ultimately, these recommendations require that instead of thinking of HEIs as separate and unique, there should be a systemic regional focus on particular issues in which there is a collective commitment to investing resources. All institutions have a shared responsibility to achieve goals for teaching, research, and service.

Consider the implications if a range of institutions (e.g., R1, community college, and technical college) alongside community partners (e.g., public schools, government, and business/industry) located in the same region engaged in multi-modal and multi-scalar work. The results could truly change the landscape of a region; however, historically some institutions have remained siloed, self-serving, and focused on aspects other than the social good.

Conclusion

A study by Federal Reserve Bank in New York found that the strongest predictor of sustained economic vitality in a region is whether or not that region has sustained human capital, like that produced by research universities (Abel & Deitz, 2009, revised 2011). HEI must focus on sustainable capacity building with a willingness to acknowledge the expertise of other entities while also exchanging proprietary knowledge so that the work can be sustained and continued in the absence of whoever contributed that knowledge initially.

This approach frees all stakeholders to constantly evolve and not become transfixed in any one way of doing things preventing innovative growth and achievement (Jacob, 2015). Change within institutions is inevitable; therefore, finding ways to sustain rural regional work must be a priority.

HEIs make a considerable contribution to the public good, through services such as health and education, which play a role in economic development of the region (Goddard, 2008). HEIs can target their teacher education program to address rural teacher shortages, as well as other rural community concerns, if they are willing to identify shared goals and develop a plan of action to achieve those goals.

Investment in rural concerns "lifts all ships" as bringing more economic opportunity to a region creates an incentive for educational attainment to meet workforce needs, as well as provides opportunities for job placement within the community, reducing brain drain on the community at large. A stronger engagement between HEIs and rural communities can be a mutually beneficial relationship for both parties that will positively improve the experiences and outcomes of rural youth.

REFERENCES

Abel, J., & Deitz, R. (2009, revised 2011). Do colleges and universities increase their region's human capital? Federal Reserve Bank of New York Staff Reports, No. 401. Retrieved February 25, 2019.

ACT. (2014). The condition of future educators 2014. *ACT*. Retrieved from http://www.act.org/content/dam/act/unsecured/documents/CCCR-2014-FutureEducators.pdf.

Alleman, N., & Holly, L. (2013). Multiple points of contact: Promoting rural postsecondary preparation through school-community partnerships. *Rural Educator, 34*(2), 1–11.

American Association of Community Colleges (AACC). (2015). AACC Home Page. Washington, DC: AACC. Retrieved February 15, 2019, from http://aacc.com.

Anchor Institutions Task Force. (2016). *Journal on Anchor Institutions and Communities*. Vol. 1. Marga Inc.

Augustine-Shaw, D. (2016). Developing leadership capacity in new rural school district leaders: The Kansas Educational Leadership Institute. *The Rural Educator, 37*(1), 1–13.

Babione, B. (2010). Rural and small community educator responses to state academic standards. *Rural Educator, 31*(3), 7–15.

Barley, Z. A., & Brigham, N. (2008). *Preparing teachers to teach in rural schools*. Washington, DC: US Department of Education.

Barnes, G., Crowe, E., & Schaefer, B. (2007). *The cost of teacher turnover in five school districts: A pilot study*. National Commission on Teaching and America's Future.

Byun, S. Y., Meece, J. L., & Irvin, M. J. (2012). Rural-nonrural disparities in postsecondary educational attainment revisited. *American Educational Research Journal, 49*(3), 412–437.

Campus Compact. (2018). Carnegie community engagement classification. Retrieved February 16, 2019 from https://compact.org/initiatives/carnegie-community-engagement-classification/.

Corbett, M. (2016). Reading Lefebvre from the periphery: Thinking globally about the rural. In A. Shulte & B. Walker-Gibbs (Eds.), *Self-studies in rural teacher education* (pp. 141–156). Switzerland. Springer International Publishing.

Cuervo, H. (2016). *Understanding social justice in rural education*. Springer.

Drabenstott, Mark. (2008). Universities, innovation and regional development: A view from the United States. *Higher Education Management and Policy, 20*(2), 43–55.

Fitzgerald, H. E., Bruns, K., Sonka, S., Furco, A., & Swanson, L. (2012). The centrality of engagement in higher education. *Journal of Higher Education Outreach and Engagement, 16*(3), 7–28.

Gass, Eric. (2005). The path to partnership: A new model for understanding University-Community partnerships. *Professional Development: The International Journal of Continuing Social Work Education, 8*(3), 11–23.

Goddard, J., & Jaana, P. (2008). The engagement of higher education institutions in regional development: An overview of the opportunities and challenges. *Higher Education Management and Policy, 20*(2), 11–41.

Hammer, P. C., Hughes, G., McClure, C., Reeves, C., & Salgado, D. (2005). *Rural teacher recruitment and retention practices: A review of the research literature, national survey of rural superintendents, and case studies of programs in Virginia.* Appalachia Educational Laboratory at Edvantia (NJ1).

Institute for Educational Leadership (2005). *Preparing leaders for rural schools: Practice and policy considerations.* Washington, DC: Institute for Educational Leadership. Retrieved from www.iel.org.

Jacob, W., Sutin, S., Weidman, J., & Yeager, J. L. (2015). *Community Engagement in Higher Education: International and local perspectives. Community Engagement in Higher Education: Policy Reforms and Practice* (pp. 1–28). Rotterdam: Netherlands. Sense Publishers. 10.1007/978-94-6300-007-9_1.

Johnson, L. (2004). Research-based online course development for special education teacher preparation. *Teacher Education and Special Education, 27*(3), 207–233.

Knapczyk, D., Chapman, C., Rodes, P., & Chung, H. (2001). Teacher preparation in rural communities through distance education. *Teacher Education and Special Education, 24*(4), 402–407.

Lock, G. (2008). Preparing teachers for rural appointments: Lessons from Australia. *The Rural Educator, 29*(2), 24–30.

Lock, G., Budgen, F., & Lunay, R. (2012). The loneliness of the long-distance principal: Tales from remote Western Australia. *Australian and International Journal of Rural Education, 22*(2), 65–77.

Maier, A., & Youngs, P. (2009). Teacher preparation programs—And teacher labor markets: How social capital may help explain teachers' career choices. *Journal of Teacher Education, 60*(4), 393–407.

Malkus, N., Hoyer, K. M., & Sparks, D. (2015). *Teaching vacancies and difficult-to-staff teaching positions in public schools.* Stats in Brief. (NCES 2015-065). National Center for Education Statistics.

Maranto, R., & Shuls, J. V. (2012). How do we get them on the farm? Efforts to improve rural teacher recruitment and retention in Arkansas. *Rural Educator, 34*(1), n1.

Maurrasse, D. J. (2001). *Beyond the campus: How colleges and universities form partnerships with their communities.* New York: Routledge.

Miller, L. C. (2008). *Valuing place: Understanding the role of community amenities in rural teacher labor markets.* Stanford University.

Mollenkopf, D. L. (2009). Creating highly qualified teachers: Maximizing university resources to provide professional development in rural areas. *The Rural Educator, 30*(3), 1–6.

Monk, D. H. (2007). Recruiting and retaining high-quality teachers in rural areas. *Future of Children, 17*(1), 155–174.

Ohlson, M., Johnson, J., Shope, S., Rivera, J. (2018). The Essential Three (e3): A university partnership to meet the professional learning needs of rural schools. *The Rural Educator, 39*(2), 1–10.

Petrin, R., Schafft, K., & Meece, J. (2012). *Educational sorting and residential aspirations among rural high school students: What are the contributions of schools and educators to the rural brain drain?* Paper presented at the American Educational Research Association annual meeting, April 2012, Vancouver, BC.

Ramsey, G. (2000). *Quality matters.* Sydney: New South Wales Department of Education and Training.

Rutheiser, Charles. The promise and prospects of Anchor Institutions: Some thoughts on an emerging field. Retrieved March 2, 2016 from https://www.huduser.gov/portal/pdredge/pdr_edge_hudpartrpt_062211.html.

Sjoberg, G. (2018). Rural-urban balance and models of economic development. In *Social structure and mobility in economic development* (pp. 235–261). Routledge.

Smith, D., & Tran, H. (2019). Teaching in rural America: Talent management, challenges, and potential solutions. In *Community college teacher preparation for diverse geographies: Implications for access and equity for preparing a diverse teacher workforce.* In Press.

Taie, S., & Goldring, R. (2017). Characteristics of public elementary and secondary school teachers in the United States: Results from the 2015–2016 National Teacher and Principal Survey. First Look. NCES 2017-072. *National Center for Education Statistics.*

Tran, H. (2018). *Taking the mystery out of South Carolina school finance* (2nd ed.). Ypsilanti, MI: ICPEL Publications.

Tran, H., Hogue, A. M., & Moon, A. M. (2015). Attracting early childhood teachers to South Carolina's high needs rural districts: Loan repayment versus tuition subsidy. *Teacher Education Journal of South Carolina, 8*, 98–107. Retrieved from: http://www.scateonline.org/pdfs/Journal.Final.2015.pdf.

Tran, H., Smith, D., & Fox, E. (2018). *The perspectives of potential and current rural teachers for rural teacher recruitment and retention in South Carolina.* University of South Carolina's Center for Innovation in Education Report. Retrieved from: https://www.usccihe.org/s/SC-Rural-Teacher-Staffing-Report.pdf.

Warren, L. L., & Peel, H. A. (2005). Collaborative model for school reform through a rural school/university partnership. *Education, 126*(2), 346–352.

Watlington, E., Shockley, R., Guglielmino, P., & Felsher, R. (2010). The high cost of leaving: An analysis of the cost of teacher turnover. *Journal of Education Finance, 36*(1), 22–37.

Weidman, J. C., Yeager, J. L., Jacob, W. J., & Sutin, S. E. (2015). *Community engagement in higher education: Policy reforms and practice.* Rotterdam: Sense Publishers.

Chapter 8

Systemic Advocacy and Stakeholder Collaborations

Supporting Students Emerging from Foster Care Who Matriculate to College

Sarah Jones

INTRODUCTION

In 2016, there were approximately 430,000 youth in the United States in the foster care system (FCS). Of this group, about 300,000 were school aged (between four and twenty years old) and could be served in the public K-12 education system or the postsecondary system (U.S. Department of Health and Human Services, 2016).

The trauma associated with transitioning into the FCS (and out of a parent or guardian's home), atop the trauma associated with the abuse and/or neglect that led for many youth to the need for an out of home placement, creates a space where barriers to academic success increase. As a result, very few alumni of foster care matriculate and then graduate from college (Unrau, Font, & Rawls, 2012). Myriad barriers to success in schools, such as multiple home and school transitions, add layers of marginalization to an already vulnerable population (Unrau, Font, & Rawls, 2012; Wolanin, 2005).

Despite their disproportionately low representation in higher education, more than 70 percent of students emerging from foster care, referred to throughout the chapter as SEFC, have postsecondary aspirations (McMillen, Asulander, Elze, White, & Thompson, 2002). This sense of hope and optimism from a group of students that has been historically underserved and overburdened creates a space for advocates, allies, and community stakeholders to learn about (and from) this population of students, collaborate with professionals across systems, and work with SEFC on micro-, meso-, and macro-levels.

Despite their aspirations, fewer than 10 percent of SEFC matriculate to college, and of those, fewer than 10 percent graduate with an associate's or bachelor's degree (Emerson, 2006; Pecora et al., 2006; Wolanin, 2005). Like their peers from other marginalized groups or identities (e.g., students of color, students from low socioeconomic backgrounds, first generation college students), SEFC have less social and educational capital, thus compounding the barriers to academic success.

Furthermore, when compared to peers with similar demographic characteristics, SEFC trail in almost every category used to measure academic success. For example, SEFC have higher percentages of absenteeism and truancy, are more likely to transition to multiple schools throughout their K-12 career, and are placed in special education classes at higher rates than their peers not in the FCS (Davis, 2006; Unrau et al., 2011; Wolanin, 2005).

Further, SEFC are less likely to be placed in college preparatory coursework and are more likely to be served by the least qualified educators (Unrau et al., 2012). Considering the trauma associated with childhood abuse and/or neglect, layered with inequitable K-12 school services, it is unsurprising that SEFC are less likely to graduate high school or earn a general equivalency diploma (Okpych & Courtney, 2014).

Consequently, most SEFC do not matriculate to college, and if admitted, researchers suggest that up to 90 percent depart before receiving an associate's or bachelor's degree (Davis, 2006; Unrau et al., 2012; Wolanin, 2005). Therefore, no other group of students is more at risk of attrition than SEFC. This chapter emphasizes the ways stakeholders can engage with each other and SEFC in order to improve the educational opportunities for some of the most marginalized students across the P-16 educational continuum.

SUMMARY OF RESEARCH

Data included in this chapter was gleaned from a phenomenological inquiry (Moustakas, 1994) regarding the educational experiences of SEFC. Students, in their second year of college or beyond, who also spent at least eighteen months in the FCS were eligible to participate and data for each of the eight participants were collected via semi-structured, one-on-one interviews.

The themes gleaned through phenomenological reduction (Moustakas, 1994) include *consequences of trauma, peer relationships, integration of social and academic experiences, and love*. These themes capture the lived experiences of participants who used their resilience to matriculate into and progress through college.

Though participants described feeling like outsiders in K-12 schools, most made meaningful connections as undergraduates. These connections with peers as well as the integration of social and academic experiences helped participants progress. Finally, participants described the love they found for themselves through their journeys in foster care and college.

SYSTEMIC DOMAINS

Sociologists and social workers have long understood the barriers associated with the FCS and the inherent inequity youth in the system encounter (Courtney & Dworsky, 2006; McNaught, 2004; Percora et al., 2006). Research has also highlighted the characteristics and resources SEFC embrace and utilize to increase their opportunities for academic success (Unrau et al., 2012).

The following paragraphs will summarize literature regarding resources and barriers for academic success using the structure and language from the American Counseling Association's (ACA) Advocacy Competencies (Toporek, Lewis, & Crethar, 2009) to organize the information. The ACA's advocacy competencies describe a process counselors use to promote systemic change. The model includes ways professional counselors act on behalf of or with clients (students) to promote change on micro-, meso-, and macro-levels. These levels will be described and included in figure 8.1.

All clients and students have interactions at the micro-, meso-, and macro-levels. From micro-level or client/student level interventions, the emphasis is

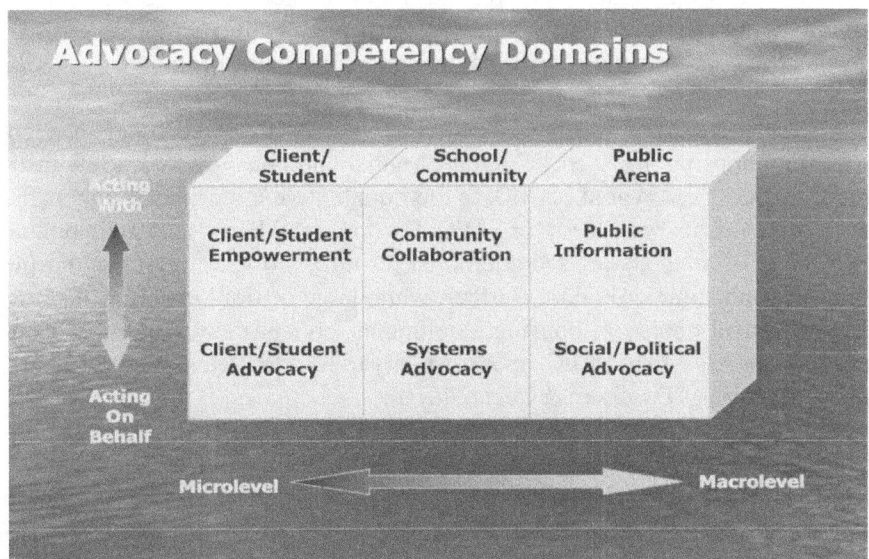

Figure 8.1 ACA's Advocacy Competency Domains (Toporek et al., 2009).

placed on the client or student. At this level, personal history, salient identity characteristics, and individual resources are key to the development of self-advocacy. Further, sociopolitical, systemic, and environmental factors impact personal experiences of clients and students. Meso-level or school and community levels highlight community collaboration and enlarge the micro-level domain to include community settings.

This system's advocacy includes ways organizations help or hinder client/student navigation at the school level. Macro-level domains expand the purview to include the public arena. This large-scale perspective includes the ways social and political structures lead to oppression and marginalization of vulnerable populations (Toporek et al., 2009).

Micro-Level Domains

Micro-level advocacy competencies emphasize the experiences of the client or student. The individual is key in this small-scale perspective. Personal necessities including physiological needs (e.g., food and safety), psychological needs (e.g., connections to others and self-efficacy) (Maslow, 1943), and cognitive and/or developmental ability are included in micro-level domains.

Access to stable housing is the most consistent micro-level barrier to P-16 academic success for SEFC (Dworsky & Perez, 2010; Nelson, Fox, & Zeanah, 2013). For K-12 students, each new home placement potentially leads to a school transition, as well. On average, SEFC make three more school transitions than their peers outside the system (Casey Family Programs, 2011), and each transition equates to a loss of up to six months of knowledge (Rios & Rocco, 2014).

Students attending postsecondary institutions also encounter barriers regarding housing. Most SEFC require year-round housing, which few institutions offer (Nelson et al., 2013). In their qualitative inquiry regarding barriers to postsecondary success for SEFC, Dworsky and Perez (2010) found that two-thirds of students needed additional resources to secure housing during semester and summer breaks. Further, while large institutions offer the most flexibility and choice in housing, community colleges and commuter campuses—schools where SEFC are more likely to be admitted—have the fewest housing options (Dworsky & Perez, 2010).

Psychological needs regarding personal identity, self-worth, and relationships with others are also micro-level areas that impact academic success. Most students want to leave behind the stigma associated with being a youth in foster care (Salazar, Jones, Emerson, & Mucha, 2016).

When youth emancipate from the system, it becomes nearly impossible for postsecondary schools to identify these students then provide resources necessary for academic success. Consequently, SEFC have a difficult time in transition (Salazar et al., 2016) and report feelings of disempowerment, marginalization, and hopelessness that increase the likelihood of postsecondary attrition (Morton, 2015).

Multiple experiences of neglect, abuse, and trauma associated with their life circumstances not only increase negative self-perception, but also increase mental health concerns (Emerson, 2006). Compared to their peers not in the FCS, youth in foster care face increased instances of post-traumatic stress (Berderian-Gardner et al., 2018). Students' experiences with depression and anxiety can be barriers to academic success.

The symptoms of depression (e.g., lack of concentration, social isolation, and suicidal ideation) are six times more likely to manifest in children and adolescents who experience social disruption (Berderian-Gardner et al., 2018; Jones, 2013). Because SEFC are in perpetual transition and have experienced significant abuse and/or neglect, they are at greater risk of having depression and/or other mental health concerns that negatively impact their academic success (Casey Family Programs, 2011).

Though much of the current research emphasizes a deficit perspective regarding SEFC (Nelson et al., 2013; Rios & Rocco, 2014), there is also research that features positive, micro-level strategies for academic success (Chambers & Palmer, 2010; Kirk, Lewis, Nilsen, & Colvin, 2013). For example, SEFC often exhibit intrapersonal strength and resilience (Rios & Rocco, 2014).

Rios and Rocco (2014) identified seven internal resiliency traits or "success strengths" (p. 332) of SEFC. They include *perseverance*, or endurance through difficulty while pursuing a goal; *responsibility*, or accountability for their academic success; *resourcefulness*, or the ability to ask for help when necessary; *diligence*, or focus and steady work on the necessary material; *motivation*, or the desire to complete specific academic goals; *goal orientation*, or the ability to move beyond short term vision to secure long term goals; and *self-efficacy*, or the belief in personal ability to be successful.

Participants in the study presented in this chapter similarly described feelings of maturity, independence, engagement, and self-love. Like participants in Rios and Rocco's study (2014), participants in this study were motivated to move beyond their circumstances. Their dedication to meeting their educational goals created a space where participants were more likely to engage in academic and cocurricular activities instead of social events that they believed would lead to drinking and drug consumption. In fact, though no question asked about alcohol or drug use, seven of the eight participants described their decision to abstain from both, thus increasing their time to engage in on-campus programming and scholastic interests.

SEFC can use postsecondary education as an opportunity to "redefine their identity" (Watt, Norton, & Jones, 2013, p. 1415). Instead of shedding their powerful traits of dedication, perseverance, and resilience (Salazar et al., 2016), SEFC have been successful in higher education when they transferred the life skills they accumulated over time to their experiences in college (Watt et al., 2013).

As these students are affirmed, they experience increased hope, confidence, and direction (Nelson et al., 2013). As SEFC gain confidence, many are able to increase their leadership development (Dworsky & Perez, 2010) and their social capital while they create connections, thus increasing the likelihood of academic success (Jim Casey Youth Opportunities Initiative, 2011).

Meso-Level Domains

SEFC are active members in at least two separate yet equally confounding systems (i.e., education and social services) that sometimes, through limited cross systems communication, tighten the web of oppression and increase barriers to academic success instead of disentangling resources to serve a common goal (Noonnan et al., 2012). Meso-level advocacy competencies move beyond self to emphasize connections and collaborations between schools and communities (Toporek et al., 2009).

As the focus shifts to include local systems, communication between systems is critical. The lack of collaboration between social services and education systems means SEFC are often left to navigate both systems independently, especially once they depart from high school. Though this transition to young adulthood is difficult for all individuals, SEFC face unique and additional systemic barriers that help maintain inequity (Rios & Rocco, 2014).

For example, SEFC lack financial capital, social networks (Watt et al., 2013), and healthy interpersonal relationships, as well as, the communication skills necessary to manage their poverty (Nelson et al., 2013). Additionally, most SEFC transition out of the FCS without a driver's license, no savings, limited cash, and inadequate knowledge and skills necessary to navigate the systems that can offer assistance (Unrau, 2011).

Though systems of education and social services have historically had difficult times advocating and empowering SEFC, meso-level strategies including campus support programs, mentoring, and collaborations between systems are promising practices that have led to academic success for SEFC.

Campus support programs that emphasize autonomy and create spaces where students have access to the scaffolded support necessary to meet the challenges of college (Watt et al., 2013) are increasing in popularity (Dworsky & Perez, 2010; Hernandez & Naccarato, 2010; Kinarsky, 2017; Watt et al., 2013).

Many programs helped students find financial resources, and others offer scholarships for attendance (Hernandez & Naccarato, 2010; Kinarsky, 2017). Other commonalities for support programs include mentoring, outreach, career preparation, mental health assessments, and general campus orientation activities (Watt et al., 2013).

There are multiple opportunities for SEFC to engage with their school and community systems (Rios & Rocco, 2014), and this engagement is an important factor in students' academic success. Each participant named at least one organization that offered a mentor or other stakeholder, outside of school, who encouraged and/or expected college matriculation, while also helping students navigate systemic and community barriers.

Rios and Rocco (2014) highlighted the phrase "education-savvy mentors" (p. 232) to describe adults outside of the educational system who have the knowledge and skills necessary to help students navigate the transition from high school to college. Community mentors, caseworkers, and foster parents can offer substantial support for the academic success of SEFC by helping students navigate the educational and social services systems (Syed, Azmitia, & Cooper, 2011).

Macro-Level Domains

Macro-level advocacy competencies encompass the public arena and frame barriers to and resources for academic success in a sociopolitical context (Toporek et al., 2009). Beyond stakeholders within their small communities, SEFC have limited support and few advocates who believe they are capable of achieving academic success. The stigma associated with the FCS and the individuals who are placed in it leads to low societal expectations for SEFC (Kirk & Day, 2011; Nelson et al., 2013).

Because of micro and meso-level barriers, SEFC form a "worldview that focused on deficits, dysfunction, and pathology" (Watt et al., 2013, p. 1410). As SEFC face greater barriers, it is up to the larger community to help shift perspective from "deficit, stigmas, and shame to one of strength, survival, and stamina" (Watt et al., 2013, p. 1415). Students who participated in this study described the toll of negative stigmas that followed them from system to system. One participant described the fatigue that set in due to her constant "hustle."

In trying to keep up with peers who have family privilege (Seita, 2014), or the (often) unnoticed benefits of a stable family, SEFC experience increased pressure to succeed not only to negate the negative stigma associated with foster care, but also because they do not have the familial support their peers have. In other words, their lack of sociopolitical capital and family privilege create an impossible situation where SEFC must succeed in whatever they are doing, just to survive.

Advocates for youth who emerged from foster care have been successful generating policy regarding postsecondary education for SEFC. Federal programs that offset the cost of tuition for SEFC help to generate equity for a marginalized population. The John H. Chafee Foster Care Independence Act of 1999 gave states discretionary funds for postsecondary education for SEFC.

In 2009, the program distributed $45 million in educational and training vouchers (ETV). ETVs provide up to $5,000 per year to offset postsecondary expenses. Students who know about the program and have not transitioned out of the FCS are eligible for an ETV. Though this act made it easy for students to receive funds until they transitioned out of the FCS at eighteen, the Fostering Connection to Success and Increasing Adoptions Act of 2008 made it easier for youth to stay in care and receive financial support until their twenty-first birthday (Hernandez & Naccarato, 2010).

Additionally, many states and private organizations provide scholarships for college expenses. For example, Texas offers tuition exemption for SEFC, as well as for those who were adopted. Casey Family Programs is a private organization that provides scholarships for SEFC (Texas Department of Family and Protective Services, n.d.). Though these programs offer substantial financial resources for youth in the FCS, they are insufficient and inadequate when not accompanied by structural social and academic support efforts (Hernandez & Naccarato, 2010).

STAKEHOLDER ENGAGEMENT

By working for and with individuals, systems, and sociopolitical environments stakeholders can collaborate with each other and SEFC to advocate and influence the social, political, economic, and cultural factors of human development. In micro-level domains, SEFC benefit from consistent assistance with competent and loving professionals who care and know enough about the K-12, undergraduate, and social service systems to share the resources and knowledge necessary to help students navigate their web of services while in transition.

In meso-level domains, stakeholders collaborate to bring change to schools and communities. Stakeholders at meso-levels can oversee systemic changes in the K-12, social service, or higher education systems by having cross organizational conversations that generate action toward the support of SEFC (Toporek et al., 2009).

In macro-level domains, stakeholders consider large systems that include the public arena and frame barriers to and resources for academic success in a sociopolitical context (Toporek et al., 2009). Professionals in K-12, social services, and higher education systems have an opportunity to collaborate, advocate, educate, and modify their practices in order to help one of the most vulnerable populations of students by engaging in professional development, sharing data, having conversations, and pooling resources.

The next section includes ways community stakeholders can collaborate within micro-, meso-, and macro-levels to benefit SEFC. Data included in this chapter is a result of a phenomenological inquiry of eight students in their second year or beyond of college, who also spent at least eighteen months in the FCS.

Their first-person narratives and experiences give a necessary voice to this work and help to explain the necessity of the resources communities can offer. For example, one student said, "I am a foster kid who doesn't have any contact with my parents; I really don't have that support but most people that I have met [not in the FCS] are completely reliant on their parents."

Foster or Adoptive Parents

Foster and adoptive parents have a critical role in the educational achievement of the children placed in their home. While some foster parents did little to cultivate the educational aspirations of the participants, others became their child's educational advocate. One participant discussed the way her foster parents made it possible for her to remain in her previous high school, creating opportunities for her to graduate with friends and avoid another school transition.

Another student, who identified as first generation said that her [foster] mother warned her of college expectations and was comforting when she did poorly her first semester. She said, "My mom told me that it's going to be different and more difficult. She wanted to prepare me. I was a steady student in high school but she wanted me to know that college was hard. I didn't understand the level of difficulty."

Participants also described the ambiguity and lack of closure when they turned eighteen; they wondered about the level of support their foster parents would offer when they went to college. Participants' experiences varied. While two participants never saw their foster parents after college move-in, others maintained relationships that participants described as critical to their academic persistence. One participant "joked about getting a tattoo of [my foster mother's] name" because the supportive relationship created a situation where the student felt secure enough to take educational risks and ultimately graduate with an associate then bachelor's degree.

Social Service Employees, Community Counselors, and Child Advocates

Myriad people work with and for students in the FCS, most of them on micro-levels. However perpetual transitions in systems generate inconsistency in support for students at micro- and meso-levels, thus creating situations where SEFC have to look in multiple places to receive advice and resources to achieve their educational goals.

Participants described having multiple case workers, community counselors, and foster homes. One participant said, "Inconsistency was the hardest thing. Having different people change all the time. 6 different case workers, three GALs, so many therapists I can't count them all. Not being able to know where your support was."

Fortunately, students who found at least one consistent adult were able to navigate their situations, receiving the support and resources necessary to transition successfully from high school and into college.

Social workers, counselors, and child advocates supported students through their educational transitions. Study participants learned about scholarships from their Chaffee workers, internships from their mentors, and life skills from their guardian ad litem. While students transitioning from high school to college who were not in the FCS were more likely to have parental support, SEFC were guided by a team of adults. One participant said, "The process of being the adult is intense and I wouldn't have done it by myself if I didn't have their support or guidance."

P-16 Employees

While teachers and school administrators do their part in encouraging students to pursue postsecondary education, SEFC look to P-16 personnel for different levels of support. In fact, students who found support from P-12 teachers, principals, and school counselors said that they were the adults who helped them write college entrance essays and gather school documents necessary to apply to college.

Further, multiple participants described the relationships they had with an educator who opened their homes when college campuses closed for winter, spring, and summer breaks. "When I'm not living in my dorms on campus, there is a teacher from when I was 11 years old whose house I go to. She's my support system."

Upon arriving in college, many SEFC have transitioned out of the FCS, thus diminishing their support system. The gap between services students receive from a team of stakeholders transitions to college campuses when the students do. On college campuses, SEFC found support via faculty, student affairs professionals, and student organizations.

The level of support was often determined by the needs of the students. When on academic probation, for example, participants found programs such as supplemental instruction and peer tutoring via their residence hall to gain the resources they needed to manage their time and meet the rigorous expectations of college life. Beyond resources, participants cited the amount of love they received on college campuses as an important factor in their academic success. One participant said:

> There's definitely a heavy amount of love. . . . It's very hard for me [as a student emerging from foster care] to make connections and actually it's one of the best bits of being here at [college]. Finding a family away from home where I can have a support system away from home is really great. I think if more foster youth had that ability or had that opportunity to actually have a group of people who really cared about them that they can go to no matter what. I think they'd do a lot better. And I think they'd be a lot more successful.

SEFC found college campuses to be safe places where they developed their identities beyond the label "foster kid." Some students were able to make new meaning from their experiences by collaborating with students and staff who cared about their academic success and understood the amount of trauma associated with their childhood and the perpetual challenges of everyday life without familial support. Other study participants marveled at the ability to find employment, housing, mental health services, and mentoring in one location.

Considering the needs of students graduating from high school, college campuses offer an array of support services, as well as the opportunity for additional education, therefore making the transition to college from high school a stable option for SEFC.

STAKEHOLDER COLLABORATION

As students from foster care engage with stakeholders there are multiple opportunities to generate working collaborations that begin at the micro-level but have implications for change at meso- and macro-levels. While the stigma associated with foster care and SEFC seems to be constantly looming throughout the sociopolitical climate, stakeholder efforts to generate educational equity begin on micro- and meso-levels.

As students in this study and others described the amount of micro-level support from professionals and stakeholders in the education and social services systems, their support was often fragmented and determinant of an individual's knowledge of one particular systems. SEFC who have been successful in college have been able to connect the pieces of micro-level support themselves.

If we are to increase the support for this population it is necessary to generate meaningful collaborations within and between systems or build new systems to generate a web of support for one of our most vulnerable student populations. Cross system collaborations are beginning in states like California and occurring in smaller capacities throughout the United States. Until students are ready and able to advocate for themselves in all three systemic domains, stakeholders have a critical role in the educational transitions.

CONCLUSION

SEFC are a vulnerable yet resilient group. Currently half of the population do not graduate high school, and less than 2 percent of the 10 percent who transition to college stay to graduate. Alumni of foster care deserve the best, and community stakeholders across the P-16 continuum can help to generate equity by working in micro-, meso-, and/or macro-level systems to educate, connect, advocate, and awaken others.

Community stakeholders, professionals, and educators can collaborate to build bridges between systems and diminish barriers to educational success. Only by working together is the knowledge and power to make change possible. When stakeholders understand students' unique perspectives and work to make changes with systems, more SEFC have an opportunity to actualize their dreams of attending and succeeding in college.

REFERENCES

Bederian-Gardner, D., Hobbs, S., Ogle, C., Goodman, G., Cordon, I., Bakanosky, S., Narr, R., Chae, Y., and Chong, J. (2018). Instability in the lives of foster and nonfoster youth: Mental health impediments and attachment insecurities. *Children and Youth Services Review, 84*, 159–167. doi: 10.1016/j.childyouth.2017.10.019.

Casey Family Programs (2011). Support success: Improving higher education outcomes for students from foster care. Retrieved from http://www.casey.org/media/SupportingSuccess.pdf

Chambers, C., & Palmer, E. (2010). Educational stability for children in foster care. *Touro Law. Review, 26*, 1103–1130. https://doi.org/10.1111/j.10990860.1992.tb00389.x

Courtney, M., & Dworsky, A. (2006). Early outcomes for young adults transitioning from out-of-home care in the USA. *Child & Family Social Work, 11*(3), 209–219.

Davis, R. J. (2006). *College access, financial aid, and college success for undergraduates from foster care.* National Association of Student Financial Aid Administrator. Retrieved from http://files.eric.ed.gov/fulltext/ED543361.pdf.

Dworsky, A., & Pérez, A. (2010). Helping former foster youth graduate from college through campus support programs. *Children and Youth Services Review, 32*, 255–263. doi:10.1016/j.childyouth.2009.09.004.

Emerson, J. (2006). Strategies for working with college students from foster care. *E-source for College Transitions. National Resource Center for the First-Year Experience and Students in Transition, 3*(4), 3–4. Retrieved from http://sc.edu/fye/esource/.

Hernandez, L., & Naccarato, T. (2010). Scholarships and supports available to foster care alumni: A study of 12 programs across the US. *Children and Youth Services Review, 32*(5), 758–766. https://doi.org/10.1016/j.childyouth.2010.01.014.

Jim Casey Youth Opportunities Initiative. (2011). Adolescent brain: New research and its implications for young people transitioning from foster care, Executive Summary. Retrieved from http://www.lawyersforchildrenamerica.org/matriarch/documents/Executive_Summary_Final_090611.pdf.

Jones, L. (2013). The family and social networks of recently discharged foster youth. *Journal of Family Social Work, 16*(3), 225–242. doi:10.1080/10522158.2013.786307.

Kinarsky, A. R. (2017). Fostering success: Understanding the experience of foster youth undergraduates. *Children and Youth Services Review, 81,* 220–228. doi:10.1016/j.childyouth.2017.08.016.

Kirk, C. M., Lewis, R. K., Nilsen, C., & Colvin, D. Q. (2013). Foster care and college: The educational aspirations and expectations of youth in the foster care system. *Youth & Society, 45*(3), 307–323. https://doi.org/10.1177/0044118x11417734.

Kirk, R., & Day, A. (2011). Increasing college access for youth aging out of foster care: Evaluation of a summer camp program for foster youth transitioning from high school to college. *Children and Youth Services Review, 33,* 1173–1180. doi:10.1016/j.childyouth.2011.02.018.

McMillen, C., Auslander, W., Elze, D., White, T., & Thompson, R. (2002). Educational experiences and aspirations of older youth in foster care. *Child Welfare, 82*(4), 475–495. Retrieved from http://www.cwla.org/child-welfare-journal/.

McNaught, K. M. (2004). *Learning curves : Education advocacy for children in foster care.* Washington, DC: ABA Center on Children and the Law: National Child Welfare Resource Center on Legal and Judicial Issues.

Morton, B. M. (2015). Barriers to academic achievement for foster youth: The story behind the statistics. *Journal of Research in Childhood Education, 29*(4), 476. doi:10.1080/02568543.2015.1073817.

Moustakas, Clark E. (1994). *Phenomenological research methods.* Thousand Oaks, CA: Sage.

Nelson, C. A., Fox, N. A., & Zeanah, C. H. (2013). Anguish of the abandoned child. *Scientific American, 308*(4), 62–67. https://doi.org/10.1038/scientificamerican0413-62.

Noonan, K., Matone, M., Zlotnik, S., Hernandez-Mekonnen, R., Watts, C., Rubin, D., & Mollen, C. (2012). Cross-system barriers to educational success for children in foster care: The front line perspective. *Children and Youth Services Review, 34,* 403–408. doi:10.1016/j.childyouth.2011.11.006.

Okpych, N. J., & Courtney, M. E. (2014). Does education pay for youth formerly in foster care? Comparison of employment outcomes with a national sample. *Children and Youth Services Review, 43,* 18–28. https://doi.org/10.1016/j.childyouth.2014.04.013.

Pecora, P. J., Kessler, R. C., O'Brien, K., White, C. R., Williams, J., Hiripi, E., & Herrick, M. A. (2006). Educational and employment outcomes of adults formerly placed in foster care: Results from the Northwest Foster Care Alumni Study. *Children and Youth Services Review, 28*(12), 1459–1481. https://doi.org/10.1016/j.childyouth.2006.04.003.

Rios, S. J., & Rocco, T. S. (2014). From foster care to college: Barriers and supports on the road to postsecondary education. *Emerging Adulthood, 2*(3), 227–237. doi:10.1177/2167696814526715.

Salazar, A. M., Jones, K. R., Emerson, J. C., & Mucha, L. (2016). Postsecondary strengths, challenges, and supports experienced by foster care alumni college graduates. *Journal of College Student Development, 57*(3), 263–279. https://doi.org/10.1353/csd.2016.0029.

Seita, J. R. (2014). Family privilege. *Reclaiming Children & Youth, 23*(2), 7–12. Retrieved from https://reclaimingjournal.com/.

Syed, M., Azmitia, M., & Cooper, C. R. (2011). Identity and academic success among underrepresented ethnic minorities: An interdisciplinary review and integration. *Journal of Social Issues, 67*(3), 442–468. https://doi.org/10.1111/j.1540- 4560.2011.01709.x.

Texas Department of Family and Protective Services (n.d.). *College tuition and fee waiver.* Retrieved from http://www.dfps.state.tx.us/404.asp.

Toporek, R. L., Lewis, J. A., & Crethar, H. C. (2009). Promoting systemic change through the ACA advocacy competencies. *Journal of Counseling & Development, 87*(3), 260–268. https://doi.org/10.1002/j.1556-6678.2009.tb00105.x.

Unrau, Y. A. (2011). From foster care to college: The Seita scholars program at Western Michigan University. *Reclaiming Children & Youth, 20*(2), 17. Retrieved from http://www.youthpolicy.org/journals/reclaiming-children-and-youth-journal-of-emotional-and-behavioral-problems/.

Unrau, Y. A., Font, S. A., & Rawls, G. (2012). Readiness for college engagement among students who have aged out of foster care. *Children and Youth Services Review, 34,* 76–83. doi:10.1016/j.childyouth.2011.09.002.

U.S. Department of Health and Human Services, Administration for Children and Families, Administration on Children, Youth and Families, Children's Bureau. (2016). *The AFCARS report: Preliminary FY 2015 estimates.* Retrieved from: https://www.acf.hhs.gov/sites/default/files/cb/afcarsreport23.pdf.

Watt, T. T., Norton, C. L., & Jones, C. (2013). Designing a campus support program for foster care alumni: Preliminary evidence for a strengths framework. *Children and Youth Services Review, 35,* 1408–1417. doi:10.1016/j.childyouth.2013.06.002.

Wolanin, T. R. (2005). *Higher education opportunities for foster youth: A primer for policymakers.* Washington, DC: Institute for Higher Education Policy.

Chapter 9

Prime Real Estate
Branding University Syllabi

Vickie Shamp Ellis, Kaylene Barbe,
Ann McNellis, and Braden East

INTRODUCTION

Syllabi are an underutilized and underappreciated source of student communication and stakeholder engagement. Though often undervalued, there is hope the course outlined in the syllabus will inspire young scholars. Higher education syllabi vary greatly in their level of standardization in messaging and communication. For example, some higher education syllabi have standard language across a division or within an academic program. Others are less standard, may contain features required by the university, but allow for individual design.

These individual elements in syllabi may contain various types of information including photos, cartoons, and/or inspiring quotations related to the course content. Regardless of design or style, a syllabus is a conceptual and practical roadmap intended to reflect the most salient features of the course being offered—the objectives, resources, and schedule.

Most professors endeavor to role model the character of their discipline. In that spirit, various types of syllabi should, to some extent, reflect and role model each unique area. For example, the professor designing a persuasion syllabus may use Toulmin's model in one section to explain what students need to achieve to be successful in the course. Some syllabi are lengthy and comprehensive, others are brief. Most include some university-sanctioned attachment or web link to institutional expectations, policies, or deadlines.

Although some students fail to carefully read course syllabi, most refer to the document throughout the semester. As students refer to their syllabi, they likely absorb, consciously and subconsciously, information, references, and symbols deemed important by the professor, so it seems natural that students would also notice references and symbols reflecting their institution's brand. According to communications agency Noir sur Blanc, a *brand* is "a set of features of an organization, symbolized by a name which, if deftly managed, creates value and influence" (Brigitte, 2009, p. 26).

A Google search (March 19, 2019) of the phrases, *why internal branding matters* (74.4 million results), *why higher education branding matters* (91.8 million results), and *why internal branding in higher education matters* (107 million results) indicates those serious about promoting their institutions are serious about successful types of promotions. Furthermore, over the past two decades as internal branding and promotion has become popular with for-profit businesses, colleges and universities have learned that they too must consider branding for their most important internal constituents, students (Whisman, 2009).

Dennis, Papagiannidis, Alamanos, and Bourlakis (2016) explained, "How universities manage the relationship with the students and how students perceive their institution's brand can have an impact on the attachment with the institution and in turn on students' intentions to engage with the university in the future" (p. 3049). Furthermore, Dennis and colleagues (2016) found stronger student association with the university brand resulted in higher student satisfaction. Since student satisfaction correlates with brand association, there is a need to increase internal branding in the academy.

Professors' efforts to role model branding through a course syllabus should be especially true for those teaching public relations courses. The course syllabus is one of the first impressions students have of their professor's approach to the discipline and provides potential space to use public relations to augment institutional connections for students.

If public relations professors believe internal branding is as important as they teach, then the professors likely take advantage of opportunities to role model internal branding for their respective universities. Furthermore, public relations professors would have a vested interest in promoting their universities. In the end, such efforts could enhance student-university identification and ultimately support retention rates (Ackerman & Schibrowsky, 2007; Belanger, Mount, & Wilson, 2002; and Belanger, Syed, & Mount, 2007).

This work assessed the level of internal university branding found in two types of course syllabi, *Introduction to Public Relations* and *Introduction to Communication* to understand ways faculty members use internal branding in their syllabi. The study hypothesized public relations professors would be more intentional about internal university branding than professors in the general communication studies discipline.

Specifically, the hypothesis expected:

H_1: College/university syllabi created for Introduction to Public Relations (IPR) courses contain more internal branding components than syllabi created for Introduction to Communication (IC) courses (H_1: $P_1 > P_2$).

H_2: College/university academic logos have greater incidence in IPR syllabi than in IC syllabi.

H_3: College/university athletic logos have greater incidence in IPR syllabi than in IC syllabi.

H_4: College/university event promotions have greater incidence in IPR syllabi than in IC syllabi.

H_5: College/university colors have greater incidence in IPR syllabi than in IC syllabi.

H_6: College/university mission statements have greater incidence in IPR syllabi than in IC syllabi.

H_7: College/university taglines have greater incidence in IPR syllabi than in IC syllabi.

Before evaluating data to determine statistical outcomes, a review of relevant literature is presented to provide context and understanding of internal public relations in general and in higher education contexts.

LITERATURE REVIEW

Studies have compared university syllabi, typically focusing on issues related to how courses are approached. Specifically, these studies have assessed syllabi for assignments and level of rigor (e.g., Graves, Hyland, & Samules, 2010), intersections of course content (e.g., Pieterse et al., 2008) and content required in the teaching of ethics (DuBos & Burkemper, 2002). While these studies addressed course content and policies, no prior literature was found addressing the potential use of internal public relations branding in course syllabi.

Internal Public Relations, Community, and Branding

Marketing to external publics (e.g., potential contacts, individuals unknowledgeable about the product, or the general population) has been the default for public relations professionals for some time. However, scholars have urged greater emphasis on the community building potential of public relations.

Hallahan (2004) defined community as people in relationship with one another, adding that organizations are communities within communities, and internal stakeholders are communities as well. Kruckeberg and Starck (2004) and Hallahan (2004) advocate using the term "community relations" rather than public relations. Hallahan (2004) states using the term "community" rather than "public" changes the tone of the profession from being more adversarial to being more collaborative.

Disregarding internal public relations and community building can be a detriment to an organization. Lattimore, Baskin, Heiman, and Toth (2012) stated, "All great external public relations begins with great internal public relations" (p. 341). The corporate world expresses this concept through terms like "internal communications," "employee communications," and "employee relations." Thousands of individuals can comprise these internal groups requiring communication and can be significant ambassadors for their organizations.

Like external public relations, internal public relations employs various tactics including internal listservs to students, meetings and events promotion, flyers, marketing materials (e.g., brochures), and newsletters (online and print versions). These materials, designed for internal circulation, typically adhere to a unified look and style determined by the organization.

In the private sector, companies and organizations utilize symbols, acronyms, slogans, and taglines to clarify and simplify the message of their group while distinguishing their message from others. This is common of twenty-first-century branding, and "corporations invest considerable time and money in public relations to support their names and logos as symbols of quality and service" (Wilcox, 2012, p. 175). Attributes such as the name, logo, graphic style, and color are just a few of the many tools at the disposal of a branding professional and should be applied to both external and internal publics.

Internal Public Relations and Branding in Higher Education

When considering public relations in higher education, the typical college or university also focuses their efforts primarily on external publics in order to meet enrollment goals. Lattimore and colleagues (2012) confirmed the external focus of universities arguing most schools practice traditional branding in contexts like viewbooks, web sites, and other publications. With this primary external focus, universities may be missing a key, internal audience—current students.

Likewise, Whisman (2009), discuss internal branding as an asset and found university communications professionals gravitate toward external audiences, with their strongest efforts on prospective students. He noted university branding professionals "think about increased enrollment and financial outcomes, and are unaccustomed to engaging faculties, staff, students and other champions of the university in the brand-building process" (Whisman, 2009, p. 368).

Once on campus, current students, the university's largest internal audience, no longer receive intentional branding materials, yet they should be considered a key group of "ambassadors" for promoting the school. Hanover Research Group addressed the necessity of full-spectrum branding, and stated student groups are becoming increasingly diverse, requiring an appropriate response from university branding and marketing efforts (Trends, 2014).

Harvest (2003) observed a similar diversification and evolution of college students' perceptions of universities by noting, "If universities and colleges want to remain competitive in today's climate, they need to adopt a customer-centric view regarding the students they admit and behave like a company that tries to satisfy its customer's needs" (p. 9). Since current students are the largest internal university consumers, proper and strategic branding is critical.

Ackerman and Schibrowsky (2007) explained universities should engage in structural bonding—the creation of dynamic student-institution associations. They argued for a type of relationship marketing seen in the corporate world and believe practices fostering psychological ties assure more loyalty. Likewise, relationship marketing was supported in Lay-Hwa's (2011) student-as-customer study. She explained consumer satisfaction develops not only in the short term but also through "repeated positive reinforcement" (p. 214).

In the end, Lay-Hwa's work contended colleges and universities could do more to facilitate better student relationships by working harder to promote "a deeply felt relational affiliation between the customer and the service provider rather than relying on the more passive approach based on relational dependency, cognitive complacency, and inertia" (p. 221).

The university must use its brand (e.g., name, logo, and mission) to "capture the essence of the value that the college provides" (Judson, Aurand, Gorchels, & Gordon, 2008, p. 57). In addition, Brigitte (2009) argued that each level of the university from administration to departments to professors to students "must all speak with the same voice" (p. 28). She continues, "It is essential to ensure consistency among positioning, identity, strategy, stated goals, communications. . . . All of these must be in line; all must work in concert to promote the same image" (p. 28).

A university's brand, an image all students must readily recognize, relate to, and know, creates an environment in which students are confident in their school and supportive of its vision. While branding can take on many tactical forms, one document all current students receive from their university each semester is the syllabus.

Syllabi as Branding Material

Students typically receive a syllabus from their professors on the first day of class. The syllabus as an outline of lectures or course information dates back to 1889; however, the purposes of the syllabus may vary from professor to professor (Parkes & Harris, 2002, p. 55). Matejka and Kurke (1994) identified four distinct purposes of a great syllabus: "a contract, a communication device, a plan, and a cognitive map" (para., 3).

Similarly, Fink (2012) argued the syllabus contains eight major themes, one of which is a "communication mechanism" (p. 2). Used to facilitate professor-student communication and vice versa, the syllabus offers potential to express an array of information. Syllabi communicate "an overall tone or personality, so a technically detailed, unimaginative, 'cold' syllabus is usually a precursor of a boring class" (Matejka & Kurke, 1994, para., 25). In addition to being a first impression, syllabi also reveal what teachers think and feel about the subject matter and students in general (Parkes & Harris, 2002).

In light of this literature reflecting community building, internal public relations, and branding in general, universities should expand their use of syllabi. This study examined syllabi as a prime communication tool for internal public relations between the university and its largest internal audience, students. The syllabus, as a document all students receive, not only may serve as the outline for a given course, but also to reinforce the university brand with the inclusion of an academic or athletic logo, college/university colors, mission statement, tagline, or promotion of college events.

Methodology

To assess differences between basic introductory public relations syllabi and basic introductory communication syllabi, an upper-tailed proportions test was applied for independent samples. Differences were considered significant for a P value less than 0.05. In late 2017, a Google search was conducted for syllabi using the search phrase "Introduction to Public Relations Syllabus" and another Google search for syllabi using the search phrase "Introduction to Communication Syllabus" and bookmarked the results for each search.

From each list, each syllabus was assessed, in order of appearance, until reaching the saturation point. Coincidentally, the saturation point was reached for both the IPR syllabi and the IC syllabi at number 67.

By conducting a preliminary review of online syllabi from a variety of disciplines and higher education institutions, five internal branding approaches appeared consistently. To those five, a sixth was added, "promotion of a college/university event" because (after six semesters of use) the approach was found to be successful at the authors' institution. Therefore, the 132 syllabi were coded for the following internal branding features: (1) academic logo, (2) athletic logo, (3) promotion of a college/university event, (4) university colors, (5) mission statement, and (6) tagline.

The *academic logo* was considered the main image projected by the institution, and the *athletic logo* was any rendering of the school mascot. The *promotion of an event* included anything from an announcement on the course schedule (special speaker or performance) to a note in the course description. The logos, college/university colors, mission statements, and taglines were confirmed as "university sanctioned features" by comparisons to the main college/university website.

Finally, some of the categories were not mutually exclusive. For example, college/university colors that were present in an academic or athletic logo were counted in both categories. Likewise, a mission statement might be displayed in college/university colors.

Based on the combined numbers from all categories, the total internal branding presence was tested. Of the six subcategories evaluated, only *academic logo* and *college/university colors* contained enough data to evaluate separately (see Hinkle, Wiersma, and Jurs, 1998). In the end, the proportions test could only be applied to H_1, H_2, and H_5.

RESULTS

Most syllabi from either introduction course did not use the internal branding features tested. Table 9.1 reveals the limited amount of data available after analyzing 132 syllabi. Beyond the analysis for the overall differences between the IPR syllabi and IC syllabi, *academic logo* and *college/university colors* were the only categories with a frequency high enough to conduct the proportions tests for independent samples.

Since the categories were not mutually exclusive, the total number of syllabi indicating the presence of internal branding is noted in the final column. Taglines, sometimes thought of as a slogan (e.g., Loyola University's "Preparing people to lead extraordinary lives"; Austin Community College's "Start here. Get there."), were almost nonexistent.

Table 9.1 Raw Data Results

	Academic Logo	Athletic Logo	Event Promo.	College Colors	Mission Statement	Tagline	Number of Syllabi with Branding
P. R.	21	1	3	19	4	4	F=25 of 66
COMM	18	1	2	14	3	2	F=22 of 66

Table 9.2 Internal Branding Proportions

	Intro to Public Relations Syllabi N=66	Intro to Communication Syllabi N=66	P value
Total Internal Branding Features	25 (37.88%)	22 (33.33%)	0.29
Academic Logo	21 (31.81%)	18 (27.27%)	0.28
College/University Colors	19 (21.21%)	14 (28.79%)	0.84

Additionally, if a special event in the division, college, or university was occurring during the semester, the syllabus was almost never used as a place to share the information. Finally, this study found only one institution (Panola College of Carthage, Texas) that used an athletic logo on both their IPR syllabus and IC syllabus.

Table 9.2 shows the proportion of internal branding present on IPR syllabi and the proportion of internal branding present on IC syllabi. Differences between internal branding on the two different types of syllabi were not found. Hence, the results failed to reject the null in hypothesis H_1, *College/university syllabi created for Introduction to Public Relations (IPR) courses contain more internal branding components than syllabi created for Introduction to Communication (IC) courses.* Again, out of the six categories (academic logo, athletic logo, institutional event promotion, college/university colors, mission statement, and tagline) only *academic logo* and *college/university colors* could be statistically tested.

In the end, the results also failed to reject the null in H_2 (academic logo) and H_5 (college/university colors).

DISCUSSION

Out of 132 syllabi analyzed, only forty-seven could be evaluated with the internal branding criteria established. Communication professors, in general, are apparently not utilizing syllabi as a public relations tool. More surprising, public relations professors who teach internal branding are not recognizing course syllabi as a platform for role modeling internal branding.

The literature review found no studies addressing syllabi as a platform for internal communication for the university. Most studies discussed only the goals and expectations of syllabi for communicating policies, resources, and schedules, as well as establishing the roles of students and professors.

This discussion considers the data in the order the internal branding features were present from least present (athletic logo) to most present (academic logo), based on the raw data. Following consideration of these featured areas, general observations related to relationship marketing and faculty's potential role are presented in the following sections.

Branding Features

Although only one institution (Panola College of Carthage, Texas) used an athletic logo on both their IPR and IC syllabus, upon further scrutiny, it was learned the college's academic and athletic logos involve the same image—a pony. It is possible the athletic logos were not utilized since athletic endeavors may be perceived as counter to academic endeavors. Perhaps this could be the brawn versus brain dichotomy playing out in class syllabi. Nevertheless, undergraduates may find athletic logos more interesting and/or more exciting than academic logos.

Event promotions were also rarely observed on course syllabi. A few mentions occurred when a special speaker or event was relevant to the course, but not to the university. This makes sense as there is not adequate room on syllabi to include all university events, which are typically communicated to students through other forums.

Nevertheless, event promotions, when limited to what each professor deems relevant, can communicate the importance of embracing opportunities beyond the classroom as important to the college experience. Moreover, a reminder on the course schedule also punctuates events as being important to a sense of community for the whole university.

Like event promotions, there were few taglines found on the syllabi, only six all together. Taglines are designed to capture a university's identity in a concise form. Bartlett (2007) explained taglines do not have as much power in highly prestigious institutions. For example, he pointed out that Yale University's tagline, "*Light and Truth*, might as well be 'Yale.' The brand needs no introduction" (para. 8). Nevertheless, he argued lesser-known institutions should highlight their taglines; most institutions fall into that "lesser-known" category.

While taglines serve to capture a university's identity in concise form, mission statements offer specifics to support the broader university goal. Perhaps undergraduates are not readily aware of their institution's mission statement. If this is the case, some level of awareness may prove to be yet another latent form of identification.

Moreover, students in courses such as *organizational communication* or *marketing* could easily compare the university's mission statement to what the textbook argues about quality mission statements. Bottom-line, some communication syllabi fail to take advantage of such dynamic connections to the curriculum. Making connections to the students' institution may help anchor both the concepts and the student's affiliation to the university.

The final factors tested in this study were *college/university colors* and *academic logo* and were the only categories with frequencies high enough to qualify for a proportions test. Perhaps professors incorporated color because altering the color of text is a simple way to add energy to the document. However, they may not consider the application as a means of overt branding.

Likewise, if professors are thinking they should include an image at the top of syllabi, they may automatically think in terms of the school's logo. Perhaps color and academic logo are the most salient features connected to the university and if any internal branding is done, that is the direct route. Nonetheless, these two features are the most important to include on any syllabus and see them as central to efforts in relationship marketing.

Relationship Marketing

The literature review indicated internal branding proved just as important as external branding for organizations across the board. Also, the findings of this study discovered students are a large, unreached internal audience. Perhaps the faculty sees university's internal communication and branding only as the responsibility of the organization's communications office (Belanger, Syed, & Mount, 2007). Faculty may resist using internal branding because such strategies may be perceived as one more invasion of the business model into academia. In other words, the faculty views students as scholars, not customers.

This antibusiness sentiment lends to embracing the philosophy advanced by Groccia (1997) that "students should realize that the university is not selling a commodity called learning but rather providing them with an environment in which to learn, to grow, and to change" (p. 2). Colleges and universities are designed to meet the diverse needs of many, and their approaches to education should reflect students and their interests—not vice versa.

Nevertheless, categorically rejecting any business practice solely because the practice has been proven to work in corporate America would not be wise. Universities, and in particular, communication studies professors, are flexible and conscientious enough to thoughtfully use internal branding efforts while interacting with students as scholars, not customers. In the final analysis, graduates should be well-educated university ambassadors, not products.

In addition to viewing graduates as university ambassadors, current students and alums as community should not be overlooked. Perhaps *consumer communities* (Kruckeberg & Starck, 2004, p. 135) offer a means to mitigate resistance to the business model with the benefits of community. Kruckeberg and Starck (2004) define a consumer community as "a group of enthusiasts who believe in the superiority of a product or service whose members individually and as a group publicly identify with this product or service" (p. 141).

While they applied this concept to products (e.g., car enthusiasts who form clubs to share and celebrate their connection to a particular car model), Kruckeberg and Starck (2004) concluded that future studies applying the concept in education and nonprofit contexts are warranted. They offered the phrase, consumer communities, as a better descriptor for moving public relations beyond its typical marketing focus. In other words, while marketing is about products or services, consumer community is about individuals as stakeholders.

Scholar-ambassadors and consumer communities can appreciate more opportunities to identify with their university. Though relationship marketing has been implemented in business for some time (Ackerman & Schibrowsky, 2007), it is also understood how this type of marketing serves as a structural, social bonding between businesses and their clients. Universities work to attract, retain, and maintain connections with students throughout the entire higher education process. If university branding serves to positively influence retention, then scholars are well served.

Faculty's Role

Finally, most academics see syllabi as a serious form of communication with students. If internal branding embellishments are present, perhaps the document is not perceived as a contract, but rather a celebration of the university offering the course. Perhaps there is a fine line there. Yet, there is also the possibility that embedding university branding is simply not on the radar of faculty, even public relations faculty, as this study's results seem to indicate.

There may also be a lack of internal communication to faculty about a need to see students as another internal audience of the university who would welcome branding features. After all, the branding may serve as a reminder of their good choice. In the end, branding in this context also serves as another way faculty can facilitate retention and participate in university communication.

CONCLUSION

In terms of role appropriation, professors may argue branding is not their job. Belanger, Syed, and Mount (2007) argue that, to the detriment of higher learning institutions, branding is often top down. They further explain to disregard bottom-up stakeholders is a "violation of the most fundamental marketing rule: always market from the market" (i.e., professors and students) (p. 181). In reality, professors brand the university with each class they teach.

If internal branding fosters loyalty which fosters retention rates and retention rates foster job satisfaction and security, then professors might want to consider taking advantage of syllabi as overlooked opportunities for branding purposes and community building. Because students are becoming increasingly diverse, shrewd, and practical (Harvest, 2003; Trends, 2014), they may require more from universities on both traditional and unorthodox branding.

Syllabi offer an effective, ubiquitous branding opportunity in terms of reaching students, and the potential of the syllabus has largely gone unrecognized. In this study, less than half of the reviewed syllabi met any criteria given, and none met all six. This absence of institutional messaging becomes problematic for universities looking to communicate their brand successfully, especially when a consistent theme in syllabi was a strict adherence to black-and-white, text-only formatting. Finally, based on the supporting literature and results, three suggestions to guide future research and exploration of this topic are provided.

First, universities should focus efforts on developing the relationship of the student body to the institutional brand. As Ackerman and Schibrowsky (2007) stated, retention is largely dependent on post-admission experiences of the student. This is against the current trend in which students and alumni receive more brand communication postgraduation than during their time in college (Whisman, 2009). Because of these findings, and the low levels of syllabi branding material present in the current study, it is easy to see that universities are not taking advantage of bottom-up branding.

Second, professors may not be cognizant of the opportunities syllabi promise, or may view university standardization as a constraint on the presentation of course material. Additionally, printing costs must be considered, especially if the document contains various colors and images. Faculty, however, plays a central role in providing a student experience consistent with the sales pitch (Belanger, Syed, & Mount, 2007).

Yet, syllabi should not morph into a billboard. Rather, universities should test the waters of syllabus branding by encouraging the inclusion of only one or two internal branding features on course syllabi. This will have virtually no impact on printing costs yet supports the notion of effectively reaching internal audiences with brand communication.

Third, future research may assess differences in private, public, large, medium, and small institutions and may conduct a comparative study in which retention rates are acquired and compared across universities implementing different syllabi sanctions. The humble syllabus may seem like the least likely place for a relationship-building opportunity. However, educators must bid for student attention in a world saturated by demands for their attention.

Ultimately, professors have an important role in providing students space for learning, reflection, and connection. If the addition of branding elements can help reaffirm students' university choice for their education, it may help get educators closer to providing a more meaningful space for learning.

REFERENCES

Ackerman, R., & Schibrowsky, J. (2007). A business marketing strategy applied to student retention: A higher education initiative. *Journal of College Student Retention, 9*(3), 307–336. doi: 10.2190/CS.9.3.d.

Bartlett, T. (November 2007). Your (lame) slogan here. *The Chronical of Higher Education.* Retrieved from https://www.igorinternational.com/press/chronhied-branding-expert-motto-slogan.php.

Belanger, C., Mount, J., & Wilson, M. (2002). Institutional image and retention. *Tertiary Education and Management, 8*(3). doi: 10.1080/13583883.2002.9967080.

Belanger, C., Syed, S., & Mount, J. (2007). The makeup of institutional branding: Who, what, how? *Tertiary Education and Management, 13*(3), 169–185. doi: 10.1080/13583880701502133.

Brigitte, F. (2009). Higher education and the challenges of communication. Noir sur Blanc Agency (White Paper). Retrieved from https://www.case.org/Documents/Browsebyprofessionalinterest/HigherEdandCommunicationEnglish.pdf.

Dennis, C., Papagiannidis, S., Alamanos, E., & Bourlakis, M. (2016). The role of brand attachment strength in higher education. *The Journal of Business Research, 69*, 3049–3057, http://dx.doi.org/10.1016/j.jbusres.2016.01.020.

Fink, S. (2012). The many purposes of course syllabi: Which are essential and useful? *Syllabus Journal,* 1(1), 1–12.

Graves, R., Hyland, T., & Samuels, B. M. (2010). Undergraduate writing assignments: An analysis of syllabi at one Canadian College. *Written Communication, 27*(3), 293–317.

Groccia, J. E. (1997). The student as customer versus the student as learner. *About Campus, 2*(2), 31.

Hallahan, K. (2004). "Community" as a foundation for public relations theory and practice. In P. J. Kalbfleisch (Ed.), *Communication yearbook, 28* (pp. 233–279). Nahwah, NJ: Lawrence Erlbaum Associates.

Hinkle, D. E., Wiersma, W., & Jurs, S. G. (1998). *Applied statistics for the behavioral sciences* (4th ed.). Boston, MA: Houghton Mifflin.

Judson, K. M., Aurand, T. W., Gorchels, L., & Gordon, G. L. (2008). Building a university Brand from within: University administrators' perspectives of internal branding. *Services Marketing Quarterly, 30*(1), 54–68. doi:10.1080/15332960802467722.

Kruckeberg, D., & Starck, K. (2004). The role and ethics of community building for consumer products and services. In M. L. Galician (Ed.), *Handbook of product placement in the mass media: New strategies in marketing theory, practice, trends, and ethics* (pp. 133–146). Binghamton, NY: Best Business Books.

Lattimore, D., Baskin, O., Heiman S. T., & Toth, E. L. (2012). *Public relations: The profession & the practice.* New York, NY: McGraw-Hill.

Lay-Hwa [Bowden], J. (2011). Engaging the student as a customer: A relationship marketing approach. *Marketing Education Review, 21*(3), 212–228.

Matejka, K., & Kurke, L. B. (1994). Designing a great syllabus. *College Teaching, 42*(3), 115–117.

Parkes, J., & Harris, M. B. (2002). The purpose of a syllabus. *College Teaching, 50*(2), 55–61.

Pieterse, A. L., Evans, S. A., Risner-Butner, A., Collins, N. M., & Mason, L. B. (2008). Multicultural competence and social justice training in counselling psychology and counselor education: A review and analysis of a sample of multicultural course syllabi. *The Counseling Psychologist, 37*(1), pp. 93–55.

Trends in higher education marketing, enrollment, and technology. (2014). Hanover Research Group. Arlington, VA. Retrieved from http://www.hanoverresearch.com/media/Trends-in-Higher-Education-Marketing-Recruitment-and-Technology-2.pdf.

Whisman, R. (2009). Internal branding: A university's most valuable intangible asset. *Journal of Product & Brand Management, 18*(5), 367–370.

Wilcox, D. L., & Cameron, G. T. (2016). *Public relations: Strategies and tactics.* Boston, MA: Pearson.

Chapter 10

Engaging Industry Stakeholders
A Case Study of Academic Assessment Practice at a Rural Agricultural Focused Two-Year College

Douglas A. Smith, Emily C. Fox, and Alexander T. Jordan

INTRODUCTION

Many postsecondary vocational education programs rely on partnerships with local industry experts to determine the specific coursework students will take to prepare them for future careers, and a key component of this partnership involves evaluation and assessment. In practice, vocational programs choose to engage industry stakeholders to participate in the assessment of student learning among broader efforts to ensure students have obtained the necessary skills to be successful before beginning work (Devier, 2002; Gruber, 2000; Kisker & Carducci, 2003; Zinser, 2003).

However, little attention has been given to the role that industry stakeholders have specifically in assessment practice within scholarly literature. For example, Kisker and Carducci (2003) comprehensively describe community college partnerships with the private sector focused on contract training, technology innovation, and workforce development broadly but omitting the role of partnership in assessment practice.

Likewise, while Devier (2002) broadly focused on the value of industry partnership in student assessment, he focused his study on an automotive programs and courses. The purpose of this chapter is to provide an empirical examination of assessment practices of a rural, vocationally focused, two-year college in the United States.

Specifically, this case study focused on understanding the role of industry stakeholders in current assessment practices to meet increasing calls for accountability for student learning. By understanding the role that industry stakeholders have in the assessment process at a vocationally focused community college, we are able to focus on and better understand the role of industry stakeholders across courses, programs, general education, and the college.

BACKGROUND

The community college is the logical source for vocational employee development and training. This is especially true in "rural areas where career training is difficult to obtain" (Zinser, 2003, p. 14) for jobs that are critically needed in the rural economies they serve (Banks, 1990; Kasper, 2002). The core mission of the American community college sector has historically focused on meeting local educational needs and building stronger community relations.

However, over time this role has expanded to include serving local businesses and industries, in addition to the individuals that live in the served communities. Howley, Chavis, and Kester (2013) accordingly describe, "Some community colleges form partnerships with local and potential businesses to provide rapid-response training or to develop degree programs that align with regional employer needs" (p. 3).

This shift in mission, beyond liberal arts and transfer, has resulted in numerous publications on how to form and maintain such partnerships (e.g., Mann, 2017; Yarnall, Tennant, & Stites, 2016). However, missing from these writings is the role industry stakeholders have in measuring the learning of students in vocational focused educational programs. This work seeks to begin to fill the gap of understanding the details of industry partnership practice for assessment in community colleges and what is currently known in the scholarly body of literature beyond the mere existence of these partnerships.

Industry Stakeholders

The symbiotic relationship between community colleges and local industry has long existed, but was reemphasized in the United States through the 1988 call from the Nationwide Commission on the Future of Community Colleges to take a leading role in developing local workforces (Kasper, 2002). Since then, movements such as the 2000 Workforce Investment Act, initiatives from the Obama administration, and the Workforce Innovation and Opportunity Act in 2014 (Brown, 2018; Kisker & Carducci, 2003) have continued to promote stronger partnerships between two-year institutions and industry.

Both community colleges and local industries have benefited from twenty-first-century collaborative efforts to develop an industry-ready workforce. As explained by Kasper (2002), community college and industry partnerships achieve the following outcomes:

> They allow community colleges to develop specific program and career fields to introduce high school students, offer a support system for the corporation involved in the partnership, provide workforce training for the local community, and enable companies to beef up employee skills through short-term training offered at the local community college. As a result of such partnerships, many community colleges have molded themselves into more comprehensive educational institutions as they increasingly cater to the workforce needs of local businesses and communities. (p. 17)

The mutually beneficial outcomes of these partnerships ensure the development of an employable workforce that has the skills necessary for industries to succeed.

In order to ensure students gain the appropriate skills by industry standards, community colleges and industries often work together in assessing and evaluating the learning of students. Current studies present examples of varying levels of engagement industries have in this process. Gruber (2003) recommends that employers outline the objectives, scopes, and outcomes for training programs, as well as participate on an advisory committee that influence the curriculum provided by community colleges.

Devier (2002) additionally explains that in an automotive technician program at Owens Community College, institution faculty and experienced external industry experts performed assessment. These joint efforts then influence any changes in curriculum and program objectives to tailor the skills students learn to the needs of local employers. This reflects that there is no one-size-fits-all approach to assessing programs, but industry stakeholders must be involved in assessment in some way to ensure students are graduating with the skills needed for employment.

Assessment

Academic assessment is the act of evaluating student learning through the systematic collection of information in order to inform decisions (Walvoord, 2010; Suskie, 2009). In higher education, academic assessment exists at the course, program, general education, and institutional levels (Suskie, 2009). Assessment at each level is important for a contemporary view of an integrated, collaborative learning experience.

Walvoord (2010) describes assessment at its core in three simple steps—goals, information, and action. *Goals* meaning the outcomes or objective students should be able to do, *information* meaning the measures or evidence collected to evaluate how well goals are achieved and what influences learning, and *action* meaning how information is used to improve learning.

A growing volume of literature addressing assessment issues in higher education exists and in recent years has begun to more thoroughly address assessment at the community college (Caudle & Hammons, 2018; Syed & Mojock, 2008). However, despite the growing call for accountability at community colleges, the current literature has failed to specifically address academic assessment at these institutions, where industry relationships are common and critical linkages to local labor markets.

For this study, academic industry stakeholder involvement in assessment was generally defined as the activities engaged in for the purpose of improving teaching and learning at all levels. This study explored assessment at Rural Agricultural College (a pseudonym), a rural two-year, associate degree granting institution located in the Midwest United States.

Theoretical Framework

The guiding framework utilized in this study was based on a model developed by the League for Innovation in the Community College's *An Assessment Framework for Community Colleges* (2004) whitepaper. It was collaboratively developed by a national panel of community college administrators and education assessment professionals. The model (figure 10.1) illustrates how the data collected through academic assessment at various levels (student,

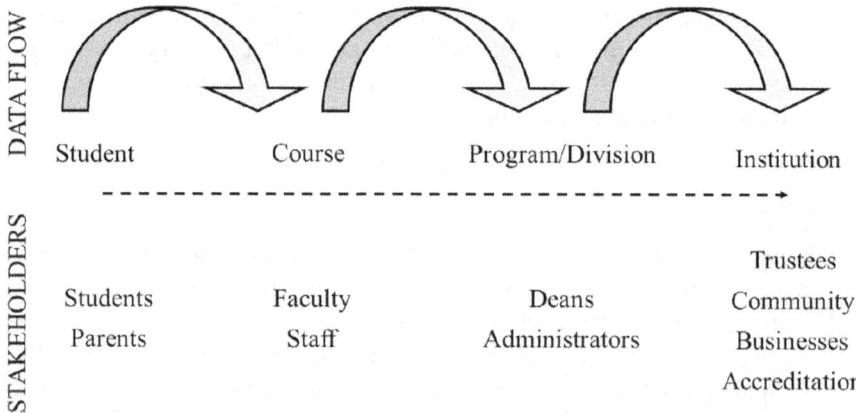

Figure 10.1 Assessment Data Flow for Institutional Effectiveness. Adapted from "An Assessment Framework For The Community College: Measuring Student Learning and Achievement as a Means of Demonstrating Institutional Effectiveness," by League for Innovation in the Community College, 2004, p. 21.

course, program/division, and institutional) informs the sequential level and who are the critical stakeholders at each level.

This model provided the foundation and a lens through which a semi-structured interview protocol was designed and the data was analyzed. The model shows how ultimately businesses who seek to hire students are stakeholders in the learning process and outcomes of students. Though businesses are not listed as a direct stakeholder in student level assessment or even at program levels, because of the flow of the assessment data collected at the preceding levels, they ultimately rely on this data to determine if students have the needed skills for employment. While it does not identify the specific involvement of stakeholders at each level, it showcases the investment each has to the process itself.

Additionally, this model identifies faculty and administrators as stakeholders in the assessment of student learning. Faculty and administrators facilitate forms of assessment and interpret the results internal to the institution. Additionally, as seen in Devier (2002), programs will partner with specific industries to determine learning outcomes. For this study, it was determined that collecting the interpretations of industry partnerships from faculty and administrators would provide valuable information to answer the research question.

METHODS

A qualitative case study method (Stake, 1995; Merriam & Tisdell, 2015) was selected to answer the central research question of:

How do persons involved with academic assessment at a rural two-year college describe assessment practice and the involvement of industry in it?

The studies four sub-questions included how does a person involved with academic assessment describe assessment practice at the (a) institutional, (b) the program, (c) the general education, and (d) course level?

A case study approach allowed for the exploration of academic assessment at a rural two-year college using a constructivist paradigm (Hatch, 2002). This approach also supported collaboration with participants to fully explore and understand the assessment process and its uses (Creswell, 2007). This case study was bounded (Creswell, 2007) to the assessment practices at Rural Agricultural College (RAC) to limit what was considered relevant to this study.

Data Collection and Analysis

Data included participant interviews and document collection used to triangulate the interview data. Documents included both publicly available sources and assessment-related documents provided by participants (e.g., college assessment plan and planning documents). Interview participants were selected following a purposeful sampling design (Hatch, 2002) to identify information rich leaders and faculty.

This study included interviewing five individuals involved with assessment at RAC. The five individuals spanned four departments, representing most of the academic areas of the college, including an administrator, program chairs, and faculty to provide a broad view of assessment.

Transcripts and documents were analyzed following Creswell's (2009) steps for analyzing qualitative data: (1) organizing and preparing the data, (2) reading through the data, (3) coding the data, (4) description and theme development, (5) interrelating themes, and (6) interpreting results. Data analysis utilized an open coding strategy (Strauss & Corbin, 1990) to identify emergent themes by breaking down, examining, and categorizing the data sources.

This included the identification of terms, descriptions, and characterizing categories to provide meaningful and relevant concepts from the data. The researchers had no prior association with any of the participants or RAC before conducting this study and have no biases or preferences toward assessment practices.

The Case

This study is situated within the overlapping contexts of the local region, the regional agricultural industry, and the two-year agricultural college located within the region. The mission of RAC is primarily focused on the development of innovative individuals for the agriculture industry and related fields.

RAC is located in a Midwest state in a city with approximately 800 residents. The nearest regional population centers are forty-five minutes away and are cities of 25,000 and 7,500 respectively. The nearest population center greater than 100,000 in population is 3.5 hours away. The regional economy is heavily focused on agricultural and specifically the strong production of beef cattle, corn, soybean, hogs, and wheat.

RAC occupies a seventy-five-acre campus including residence halls, a livestock teaching center and arena, a horticulture complex and greenhouses, an agriculture equipment complex, agriculture production and veterinary technology complex and animal holding, and an adjacent 500-acre farm for field labs.

RAC is a public two-year college operated under the state university system and closely associated with the state flagship university through its agriculture institute. Although associated with the flagship university, RAC is funded directly by the state legislature with its own line item budget and is operated autonomously from the flagship university. It is the only agricultural two-year college in the study state. Assessment is executed exclusively by RAC without interference from the flagship university.

RAC offers the Associate of Science and Associate of Applied Science degrees in four program offerings: Agribusiness Management Systems, Agriculture Production Systems, Horticulture Systems, and Veterinary Technology Systems. Within each program, several specialized options are available including a transfer option. RAC is accredited by the Higher Learning Commission, a commission of the North Central Association of Colleges and Schools. The veterinary technology program has also received accreditation by the American Veterinary Medical Association.

Participants

This study involved document analysis and in-depth interviews with five individuals involved with assessment at RAC. The five individuals spanned four departments, and included an administrator, program chairs, and faculty to provide a broad view of assessment. Dr. Terry Brown is the administrator responsible for overseeing the assessment process at RAC. Dr. Brown reports directly to the dean of the college, which is the top administrator at the school. With an education background and a PhD in agriculture education, Dr. Brown has teaching experience at both the high school and community college level and has experience starting an agriculture program at a Midwest technical college. Dr. Brown has only worked at RAC for three months.

Professor Chris Young is the chair of the general education program and has worked at RAC for three years and has been chair for a year and a half. Professor Young has master's degrees in English and History. When Professor Young first arrived at RAC he was hired to teach basic writing classes, composition, business and technical writing, and a few general education courses in history as part of the agribusiness management department. After an accreditation team visit, the college made the decision to create a separate general education department at which time Professor Young was appointed chair as the only faculty member at the college with graduate education in general education areas.

Professor Steven Chase has been a faculty member at RAC for thirty-eight years and has been the chair of the agriculture production program for approximately five years. Professor Michael Parker has been at RAC for two years and has been the chair of the horticulture program for one year. Professor Parker came to RAC after completing bachelor's and master's degrees with a horticulture focus and left graduate school knowing he wanted to focus on a career of teaching.

Professor Kathy Bell is a second-year faculty member in the horticulture program and came to RAC after completing bachelor's and master's degrees in horticulture. Initially planning to enter industry employment, Professor Bell has found that she enjoys education and teaching and plans to stay. Most faculty members at RAC have a master's degree as their highest degree earned. Dr. Brown was the only participant in this study with a terminal degree.

FINDINGS AND INTERPRETATION

Data analysis revealed two major themes that included (a) institutional assessment for consistency and industry input and (b) academic program assessment via cumulative projects and employer feedback. Both of these themes are presented and discussed with subthemes in further detail in the following sections, while highlighting excerpts from research participants and in light of the theoretical framework posited in this study, which was based off the work conducted by the League for Innovation in Community Colleges (2004).

Institutional Assessment for Consistency and Industry Input

Institutional level assessment at RAC primarily consisted of (a) aggregating program level outcomes, (b) administrative organization and guidance of assessment from a campus-wide assessment committee, and (c) a community advisory. The institutional assessment model in practice at RAC represented a continuous cycle approach that incorporated (a) methods of assessment, (b) collection of data, (c) analysis of data, and (d) implementation of changes, while integrating the mission and values of RAC to inform academic programs.

A central hub. Institutional assessment was commonly described by participants as a means to provide oversight and bring together program level assessment results and other reports facilitated by a campus-wide assessment committee. Public and industry accessibility to assessment information was stated as an important component of institutional assessment, and the college website served as the centralized hub of information for the assessment process, student learning outcomes, reports, and data. As one program chair explained, "consistency is needed to strengthen assessment and begins at the institutional level." However, he added,

> A challenge in creating consistency is getting all of our departments collecting some kind of assessment data on their program as a whole and then looking at the whole college, support services, and student services to look at the big picture.

To illustrate issues with using data to inform decisions, it was reported that, for example, student surveys had been collected for most classes at the institution, but these had not been tabulated on a consistent basis for reliable institutional use.

At the time of this study, the program chairs and the administrator responsible for assessment met as the campus-wide assessment committee to prioritize institutional items considering the strategic plan and goals. This resulted in the development of some common items and documents used campus-wide as part of assessment efforts in programs and courses. Assessment was further managed at the institutional level through regular program reviews by a separate college academic council to discuss the status of programs and industry needs.

Industry meetings and advisory councils. It was required at RAC that programs regularly meet with industry professionals and make visits to other agricultural programs as part of the assessment process. While many study participants highlighted the value of staying knowledgeable of industry needs and best practice in higher education through meetings and site visits, one faculty member expressed concern that some of these items were taking away from teaching:

> Every department has this schedule they follow to meet with industry professionals and get feedback, to go visit another institution and see what they do, etc. I'm planning to go visit another institution and talk to people and see what they are doing, but that's time consuming. It seems like it's going to interfere . . . to cancel my classes for a day or two, I think the priority is in the classroom.

Program advisory councils, composed primarily of industry professionals, served as a formal connection to industries at both the program level and the institutional level to supplement individual informal meetings with experts. Administrator Dr. Terry Brown provided an example of the usefulness of industry connections and feedback at the institutional level:

> The chief administrator of the state Farm Bureau was here and talked to us and said he was on a farm in the spring as they were getting ready to plant corn and said there were seven people around the tractor and planter. Only one or two of them were employed by the farm, the others were techs there to make sure the calibration of the planter was correct, to make sure the GPS was hooked up right—the seed rep to make sure the seed placement and all that stuff was happening, along with an agronomist. There were all these techs there to support production agriculture. When I heard this I thought that's something we need to talk about here. Are we teaching this in our classes or is it important enough that we need to have an agriculture technician program to go out and support production Agriculture?

Agricultural industries can change rather quickly and ongoing communication with industry professionals is necessary informally outside of yearly program advisory meetings to keep programs current to industry needs.

Academic Program Assessment via Cumulative Projects and Employer Feedback

The findings identified that the culture of academic program assessment at RAC centered on cumulative projects and employer feedback. Interviewees reported that most of the program assessment was performed by the program chair and had come to focus over the past ten years to involve documenting and gathering feedback from within each division, students, industry professionals, standardized testing, and the use of a capstone and portfolio.

One participant described the primary source of program assessment as "summative evaluations at the end of the program to measure student competency of the objectives and whether they are prepared to enter the workforce." A program chair added, "Assessment is assuring that we get feedback and try to then incorporate it into current classes and launch new classes; constantly revising our curriculum and how we look at things and staying in tune with what's needed."

The veterinary technology program, accredited by the Veterinarian Medical Association, was the only program at RAC that had a national board test that students must complete. These test results were used to assess the veterinary technology program. While veterinary technology used board results, other programs relied more heavily on rubrics, developed for both the program and course levels of assessment, to provide guidance on learning outcomes and objectives. Program level assessment was the most documented level of assessment with plans publicly available on the RAC website used to triangulate information provided by participants in this study.

Capstone and portfolio. Capstone and portfolio assessments served as a cumulative assessment of student learning at the program level for three of the four programs at RAC, veterinary technology utilized national board test results. The capstone was a required major course taken in the second year in which students generally, as one participant described, "do a project to develop a business plan for an operation they would like to manage or own at some point in time." Professor Chase described the capstone as:

> For example, in animal productions systems students may do an assessment like a whole ranch analysis doing budgeting, marketing, cow-care, calf-care—putting that plan together bringing all the skills from other classes, all the competencies they have met, and bringing it to a higher level to understand how it all works together.

Similarly, Professor Parker described the horticulture capstone as:

> For example, turf students will have a yearlong calendar—the maintenance they are going to be doing on the golf course or the sports fields, baseball, football fields they're working with. It's something I believe needs to incorporate practically every class that they've taken here—even sales, technical writing, and communication.

Another program chair believed that capstones measure some outcomes fairly well, but they were very subjective in many ways when trying to quantitatively evaluate them. In response to this concern, a committee approach to capstone evaluation was being tested within some programs to include individuals from within the institution and some from industries representatives.

Professor Parker noted that "the capstone should be something 'true to life' and it should be the ultimate culmination of two years here—they should have a project that encompasses everything." He also added that the goals and outcomes for the capstone were established looking at the coursework and real-world applications after graduation in consultation with industry stakeholders, "If this were just your sophomore year at a four-year college you could do more just based on coursework, but coming out you've got to have them ready to deal with what's out there." With limited credit hours, programs must provide students with career relevant instruction from day one of enrollment for students to be in a position after two years to successfully demonstrate competency in their programs.

One criticism of the capstone expressed by a program chair was "whether the capstone project was really doing what we want it to do." The chair further explained that each of the four program areas at the college is so broad and the options within each program differ greatly to the extent that each option within the programs should really be treated differently.

As a response to this criticism, Professor Chase reported that the agriculture production systems program replaced the capstone with a portfolio for equine students within the last year. He explained that "the capstone project was not measuring what they had done because it is a business plan with a lot of financial analysis and our students in the equine program are not geared towards the business side." He felt like equine students were not putting enough effort into the capstone and the capstone was not accurately measuring what they had learned and what they would do after graduation.

The portfolios required the students create a notebook documenting work they had completed through the program. The evaluation of the portfolios was still being developed at the time of this study since the students that are piloting the portfolio had not finished the two-year program yet. Professor Chase explained that if the results and experience are positive from the pilot use of the portfolio it may turn into a "good substitute for at least some of the students for the capstone project."

Student and employer feedback. Direct feedback from students and employers was found to be as a significant source of information for program assessment. Dr. Brown explained that the program advisories provided feedback on program goals and outcomes from industry professionals and employees. Professor Chase added that the advisory committee for the agriculture production program, for example, had members specialized in the areas of equine, agronomy, cattle, and hogs to provide feedback for each specialization within the program—a total of around twenty-five members.

The agriculture production programs relied on surveys of students and surveys of internship employers to provide direct feedback. Even though several program chairs explained they struggled with response rates from surveyed graduates and general permanent employers, the responses that had been received were valuable. Without industry and employer feedback, Professor Parker may not have been able to recognize as quickly the need to develop "green" curriculum.

As movement occurs within industries, program chairs actively received both formal feedback from advisories and informal feedback from graduates and employers regarding potential curriculum changes. This demonstrated a commitment from the college to engage employers in the assessment process from the beginning to the end of the assessment cycle and at various points in-between.

DISCUSSION

Assessment existed at the course, program, general education, and institutional levels, aligned with the theoretical framework for this study. These four types of assessment remained present throughout the findings of this case study. In this study participants described several overarching commonalities of the assessment process at RAC.

First, academic assessment at the college was young and was still developing in many aspects. This was apparent through the data and interviews and the description of the assessment processes as participants recognized that assessment was still gaining traction and would require continuous improvement. Assessment plans were currently in place, primarily starting at the program level, but little formal data and results had been gathered to date.

Similar to model in figure 10.1 of the theoretical framework, the influence of student feedback extended beyond the course all the way to the institutional level, and it changed how RAC served its students, even if that feedback was provided in an informal setting. As assessment plans continue to collect data for formal evaluation, the role of informal feedback from students may change and be reevaluated as more of a balanced approach to continuous improvement.

Second, participants identified assessment at the program level most regularly, although participants still recognized the role of assessment at other levels (i.e., course, general education, and institutional). Program assessment was the most planned out level and the published assessment current documents broke down results by programs.

Third, assessment was formalized to an extent through the institutional planning and the program assessment plans that had been put into place, but assessment was in a large part still informal in many of the actual assessment activities. The informal activities of assessment, such as informal conversations and feedback, were described as providing valuable qualitative information; however, this information had not been well documented.

Across all themes, informality was the most common pattern and could likely be related to the resource issues. While informal assessment results were widely described to be used in decision-making, it was difficult to discern through participants or documents the level of consistency in the use of informal assessment results to proactively inform decisions or if these results were being used to reactively justify decision-making.

Lastly, the agricultural focus of the college influenced assessment practice. By having to keep pace with the agricultural industry and the rapid changes that oftentimes occur in various industries in general, community colleges must consistently assess the programs being offered in order to prepare students to enter the industry as prepared professionals.

Unlike the framework proposed by the League for Innovation in the Community College (2004), the agricultural industry is more involved at lower levels of assessment, such as at the course level. Assessment relied heavily on employer feedback and applied student learning. Assessment at all four levels was viewed as a critical component to improve the quality of degree programs provided to increase student success.

IMPLICATIONS FOR PRACTICE AND RESEARCH

The implications and recommendations of this study have provided a starting point to describe industry involvement in academic assessment in a setting that has been largely unaddressed in previous assessment literature. Industry involvement in various levels of assessment (student, course, program, and institutional) provides the primary benefit of linking current industry standards, needs, and expectations to the skill and knowledge delivered through college programs and courses.

This is especially beneficial for vocational colleges located in small labor markets where the demand for trained employees is high and the supply is relatively limited, thus industry stakeholders have added incentive to commit time to aiding in academic assessment at a college.

Industry involvement in assessment practice centers the importance on applied skills and performance rather than memorized knowledge. At RAC, much of the assessment taking place is subjective rather than objective. Considering this, concerted efforts should promote to faculty the value of using standardized measures (e.g., rubrics) to evaluate outcomes on individual learning assignments. To supplement end of program portfolios and capstone experiences, ongoing (within and across course) measures should be further developed that align with these end of program outcomes.

Future research regarding rural agricultural focused community colleges and assessment is needed to fill the distinct lack of research on assessment in general at community colleges, but particularly at rural community colleges and the vital role of industry partners. It would behoove community college researchers to focus their efforts on best assessment practices to invoke positive changes based on empirical data at the course, program, general education, and institutional levels. This work is especially needed considering that community college are often held to the same accountability demands as colleges with more human and financial resources.

Additionally, there is a lack of research on community colleges that have industry-focused missions such as RAC. Understanding the relationship between the community college, industry organizations, and universities can assist with more robust assessment practices. Future studies should examine best practices for assessment in competency-based degree and certificate programs as well as the impact of inter- and intra-faculty communication regarding assessment.

Likewise, this work is limited by its focus on faculty and administrator perspectives on industry involvement as insiders to assessment practice. The full picture of assessment practice should expand to capture additional perspectives to include industry stakeholders themselves.

Finally, additional research on two-year colleges that operate under four-year institutions is needed. While these colleges are relatively small in number, building upon the findings of this study, more empirical research is needed to better understand the operation of these institutions, especially when provided limited human and financial resources. These recommendations would help inform decision-making and further attempt to fill gaps in the empirical literature.

CONCLUSION

Assessment is a time-consuming and often arduous process, but the data retrieved from conducting assessment can impact every level of a college or university from the student to the institution as suggested in the theoretical framework. This study helps in understanding the importance of industry partnerships in assessment practices at a small agricultural focused two-year college and within its localized context.

However, future research is needed to further explore the role of industry stakeholders in academic assessment in greater detail and across more settings. Future research should capture more full and part-time faculty perspectives on assessment and industry involvement in it and on a single level of assessment (e.g., course and program) rather than assessment practice broadly.

It is worth noting that assessment practice at RAC was limited by human capital capacity to produce and publish measurable assessment data to demonstrate student learning and teaching improvement. The results of industry involved assessment practices would be valuable data for continuous improvement data and also to aggregate for public publishing when appropriate as a way to demonstrate accountability for student learning.

Additionally, for vocational degree programs that require an internship, the opportunity to engage industry intern hosts in assessment beyond simple surveys and feedback forms is an underutilized practice and under-researched area in vocational program assessment.

In summary, assessment at community colleges, particularly rural vocationally focused community colleges, can yield impactful results at all levels during a time when institutions face greater demands for transparency and accountability. More attention and research focus must be placed on these institutions and their industry stakeholders in order to discover and relay best assessment practices.

Lastly, assessment partnerships between industry and faculty can be mutually beneficial, both formal and informal. By creating a connection and relationship between the two entities, faculty will become cognizant of industry needs and adjust their pedagogy accordingly.

REFERENCES

Brown, K. (2018). *Powerful partners: Businesses and community colleges. How investments in sector partnerships can help our economy thrive.* Washington, DC: National Skills Coalition.

Caudle, L., & Hammons, J. O. (2018). Strategies for increasing faculty involvement in institutional or program assessment. *Community College Journal of Research and Practice, 42*(1), 49–61.

Creswell, J. W. (2007). *Qualitative inquiry & research design: Choosing among five approaches*. Thousand Oaks: Sage Publications.

Creswell, J. W. (2009). *Research design. Qualitative, quantitative, and mixed methods approaches*. Thousand Oaks: Sage Publications.

Devier, D. H. (2002). Corporate partnership student assessment: The Owens Community College experience. *Assessment Update, 14*(5), 8–10.

Hatch, J. A. (2002). *Doing qualitative research in education settings*. New York: State University of New York Press

Howley, C., Chavis, B., & Kester, J. (2013). "Like human beings": Responsive relationships and institutional flexibility at a rural community college. *Journal of Research in Rural Education, 28*(8), 1–14.

Kasper, H. T. (2002). The changing role of community college. *Occupational Outlook Quarterly, 46*(4), 14–21.

Kisker, C. B., & Carducci, R. (2003). Community college partnerships with the private sector—organizational contexts and models for successful collaboration. *Community College Review, 3*(31), 55–74.

League for Innovation in the Community College. (2004). *An assessment framework for the community college: Measuring student learning and achievement as a means of demonstrating institutional effectiveness*. Chandler, AZ: Author.

Mann, E. (2017). *Connecting community colleges with employers: A toolkit for building successful partnerships*. Washington, DC: Brown Center on Education Policy.

Merriam, S. B., & Tisdell, E. J. (2015). *Qualitative research: A guide to design and implementation*. Hoboken, NJ: John Wiley & Sons.

Stake, R. E. (1995). *The art of case study research*. Thousand Oaks, CA: Sage Publications.

Strauss, A., & Corbin, J. M. (1990). *Basics of qualitative research: Grounded theory procedures and techniques*. Thousand Oaks, CA: Sage Publications.

Suskie, L. (2009). *Assessing student learning: A common sense guide*. San Francisco: Jossey-Bass.

Syed, S., & Mojock, C. R. (2008). Assessing community college student learning outcomes: Where are we? What's next? *Community College Journal of Research and Practice, 32*(11), 843–856.

Walvoord, B. E. (2010). *Assessment clear and simple: A practical guide for institutions, departments, and general education* (2nd ed.). San Francisco: Jossey-Bass.

Yarnall, L., Tennant, E., & Stites, R. (2016). A framework for evaluating and implementation of community college workforce education partnerships and programs. *Community College Journal of Research and Practice, 40*(9), 750–766.

Zinser, R. W. (2003). Evaluation of a community college technical program by local industry. *Journal of Industrial Teacher Education, 40*(2), 51–64.

About the Authors

Alan J. Brokaw, PhD, is Professor Emeritus from Michigan Technological University. He received his PhD in marketing from the University of Michigan. His research interests have included voter decision-making and marketing in Estonia. He has been a tax-paying resident of the Houghton-Portage Township School District for over forty years.

Alexander T. Jordan, PhD, is a financial aid administrator at Ashland University in Ohio. His research interests include community college student support and specifically issues related to military veteran students.

Ann McNellis, MA, is an adjunct professor at Oklahoma Baptist University focusing on classes in public relations, communications and advertising. She received her master of arts in mass communications from Texas Tech University, and worked in the PR industry for more than a decade before returning to her alma mater as an adjunct. She has taught for more than ten years and has developed courses in nonprofit public relations and social media communications.

Charles L. Lowery, EdD, is an associate professor of educational studies at the Ohio University in the Department of Educational Studies. He specializes in the work and identity of educational leaders as moral democratic agents. His major research interests focus on the relationship of critical theory to educational leadership.

Cheryl L. Burleigh, EdD, retired after twenty-seven years of experience in the field of education as a middle and high school educator and administrator both internationally and in the San Francisco Bay area, holding various administrative positions ranging from dean of student services to dean of academic and faculty affairs. She has worked in public, charter, private secular, and international schools in Luanda, Angola, and Lagos, Nigeria. Her academic research interests include ethical decision-making, education law, empowering female students in STEM, curriculum, school leadership, education equity and LGBTQ issues, and comparative education. She is a research fellow for the Center for Educational and Instructional Technology Research (CEITR) at the University of Phoenix.

Connor Fewell, MEd, is a doctoral student in the Ohio University Gladys W. and David H. Patton College of Education's Educational Administration program. He holds a MEd from the Critical Studies program in the Department of Educational Studies.

Douglas A. Smith, PhD, is an associate professor of Community College Leadership and Higher Education at Iowa State University. Dr. Smith has led community college leadership preparation programs in South Carolina and Iowa. His research is focused on contemporary community college issues, community college leadership, and rural education.

Denver J. Fowler, EdD, is the author of the best-selling book titled *The 21st Century School Leader: Leading Schools in Today's World* (Word & Deed Publishing, 2018). A former award-winning practitioner, Dr. Fowler is currently Program Chair, Doctor of Education in Organizational Leadership at Franklin University and Department Chair, College of Education—Urbana University.

Emily C. Fox, MS, is the academic project coordinator for the South Carolina Technical System and a doctoral student at the University of South Carolina. Her research interests include access and retention, community college leadership development, and women in career and technical education.

Emma Bullock, PhD, is an assistant professor of mathematics and mathematics education at Sam Houston State University. She specializes in the intersection between student mathematics achievement and school leadership particularly through the lens of Complexity Theory. She also studies teachers' use of digital math apps to afford student mathematics learning through the lens of affordances theory.

Erin L. Merz, MA, is the Director of Marketing and Communications in The School of Business at Portland State University. She received her master of arts in communications from the New York Institute of Technology, holds her Accreditation in Public Relations and serves on the Public Relations

Society of America Oregon Board of Directors. She completed grades K-12 in the Houghton-Portage Township School District.

Henry Tran, PhD, is an assistant professor at the University of South Carolina's Department of Educational Leadership and Policies and director of the Talent Centered Education Leadership Initiative (TCELI) and studies issues related to education human resources (HR) and finance. He holds two national HR certifications and serves on the board of advisors and board of trustees for the National Education Finance Academy. In addition, he is the editor of the *Journal of Human Resources*, formerly *Journal of School Public Relations*.

James F. Lane Jr., EdD, served thirty-eight years as a public school educator. His roles included high school English teacher, language arts supervisor, and middle school assistant principal and principal. He now devotes his time and energy to educational research and writing. His interests include qualitative research, specifically narrative inquiry and autoethnography. He is a research fellow for the Center for Educational and Instructional Technology Research (CEITR) at the University of Phoenix.

Kaylene Barbe, PhD, is a professor of Communication Studies, and holds the Frank W. Patterson Professorship in Communications at Oklahoma Baptist University. She teaches political communication, conflict management, and intercultural communication, and has research interests in popular culture, rhetorical criticism, and political language.

Michael E. Hess, PhD, is an assistant professor of educational studies at the Ohio University in the Critical Studies program and director of the Gladys W. and David H. Patton College of Education Honors Program. He studies issues related to social justice, rural education, democratic leadership, and qualitative methodologies.

Patricia Moyer-Packenham, PhD, is Professor and Director of the Mathematics Education and Leadership Programs at Utah State University. Her research focuses on mathematics representations and tools (including virtual and physical manipulatives), and she leads an active multidisciplinary research team made up of faculty and graduate students. Moyer-Packenham has served as PI or Co-PI on numerous research and teacher development projects totaling over $17 million in grant funding.

Rita J. Hartman, EdD, retired as a middle school principal after thirty years in public education. Along with numerous administrative and curriculum-related responsibilities at the K-12 and university level, she was a classroom teacher, a math and science teacher, and served as an instructional coordinator and instructional evaluator for a statewide Career Ladder Program. Qualitative research, specifically case study and narrative inquiry, is her current area of research and writing. She is a research fellow for the Center for Educational and Instructional Technology Research (CEITR) at the University of Phoenix.

Rowda Olad, MEd, is a district commissioner at the Benadir Regional Administration of Somalia. She holds a Masters of Education degree from the program of Counseling and Higher Education in the Gladys W. and David H. Patton College of Education at the Ohio University.

Sarah Jones, PhD, is an Assistant Professor of Professional Counseling and College Student Affairs. She teaches in the College Student Affairs and Higher Education Administration programs. Before graduating from the University of Georgia with a degree in Counseling and Student Personnel Services, Sarah worked as a classroom teacher for 10 years in North Carolina Public Schools then as an administrator in higher education where she worked with students transitioning from high school to college. Her research emphasizes the educational experiences of students emerging from foster care, particularly the matriculation, retention, progression, and graduation of this group of students.

Steven Yeager, MEd, is a college and career readiness teacher at Heath High School in Heath City Schools, Ohio. He graduated from the Ohio University Gladys W. and David H. Patton College of Education with a master's degree from the Critical Studies program.

Theresa Harrison, MPA, is a doctoral student at the University of South Carolina's Department of Educational Leadership and Policies and serves as a project manager at the Carolina Family Engagement Center in the UofSC College of Education.

Thomas E. Merz, PhD, is a professor of economics in the School of Business and Economics at Michigan Technological University. He received his PhD in economics from the University of Pittsburgh. His primary research interests include municipal and school district finances and referendums. He has been a tax-paying resident of the Houghton-Portage Township School District for nearly forty years.

Tracy Kondrit, BSEd, is a graduate of the Gladys W. and David H. Patton College of Education at Ohio University with a Bachelors in Middle

Childhood Education. While at Ohio University she was a Patton College of Education Honors student and a Cutler Scholar. She is currently a 2020 Fulbright Teaching Assistant in Malaysia.

Vickie Shamp Ellis, EdD, is a communication studies professor and the chair of the Division of Communication Arts at Oklahoma Baptist University. She serves as the communication studies research professor working alongside undergrads as they develop original projects dealing with a wide range of topics and methodologies. Her own research interests include persuasive recruiting acts in higher education, strategies for recruiting homeschoolers, and admissions discourse.